Distant Winds

By the author of the world bestseller

"THE DOLPHIN – Story of a dreamer"

SERGIO BAMBAREN

© Sergio Bambaren Roggero 1999

Cover & Design © by Sylvia Figl

Photographs by Private & Pexels

All rights reserved. No part of this publication may be used or reproduced, stored in a retrieval system, or transmitted, in any form or by any means, electronic, mechanical, photocopying, recording or otherwise, without written permission except in the case of brief quotations embodied in critical articles and reviews.

To Gail, for all the beautiful memories.

Do not follow where the path may lead.

Go, instead, where there is no path,

and leave a trail.

Anonymous

Author's Note

It was a question I heard more than once, after writing "The Dolphin" and "Beach of Dreams." What happens now, Sergio? What comes next?

I answered that I'd written all I had to. I'd told the story of a special friend I'd met while surfing in the solitude of my beloved sea, a friend who showed me that the most important thing in life is to follow your dreams. I had also written the story of a wise man I met a long time ago, one who had revealed the secrets of true happiness to me.

I was 37, and most of my time was devoted to studying and preserving the oceans and their creatures. I truly believed I'd said all I had to, and that my days as a writer were over.

But then something happened. The more I got involved in surfing and swimming with dolphins, the more I felt that voice coming from within, whispering thoughts that I knew I had to put together and share with others. So "Distant Winds" was born, in the form of a sailing boat.

I am increasingly convinced that people are bound to realize the importance of following their dreams. Only then will their uniqueness become evident to others because of their actions. That's what the librarian, Mr. Blake, taught me: that the journey of self-discovery starts within and ends in the things we do to enrich others' lives. Only by giving and learning to receive do we sincerely positively interact with others.

Based on my own life experience, I can guarantee you that we are as big as the dreams we strive to achieve. That no matter what we hear or experience with others throughout this journey called life, if we pursue our goals with all our heart, we will give real meaning to our lives. We will almost certainly accomplish what we first set out to achieve. This I learned while sailing through the South Pacific, also knon as "God's corner," with Gail, who dared to handle some of the worst storms I´d ever seen.

We only live once. But we can live this unique life we have been blessed with in such a way that at the end of the journey, we will feel as though we have lived thousands of lives.

This purpose, I believe, is what we should strive for with all our strength.

PROLOGUE

I carefully closed the cabin door of our sailing boat. The early sun wouldn't disturb Gail, who had finally fallen asleep. Twelve hours of storms had pushed us to the limit. When I opened my eyes to a peaceful Bay of Auckland, sunlight peeking through tall green mountains, its golden rays gleamed and danced across the quivering waters. Hundreds of birds high in the sky, swooping and soaring, it was hard to believe how peaceful the bay looked.

We'd lose most of our belongings in the storm, which hit as we tried entering Auckland Bay. With winds pelting our eyes and throats with salt-water and making us nearly blind, Gail and I had somehow hung on with all our strength to "Distant Winds" the beloved sailboat that had taken us on a magical journey through the South Pacific.

We'd tossed every piece of furniture and most of our belongings overboard to help ""Distant Winds"" stay afloat. The pumps couldn't keep up with the water filling the cabin of our boat.

Our lives had flashed before our eyes. But, even through our struggle against nature's wrath, we managed to hold on to the most precious belonging of all, the one we'd promised to hold on to throughout the journey. Now, tired, hurt, and almost out of strength, I stared at the old wooden box secured that held our treasure, fastened closed by a golden lock.

I carefully wiped it with a soft cloth to prevent salt-water from getting in, pulled off the string tied around my neck, gazed at the key. It seemed as though sunlight was being channeled through the green stone at the top. I held my breath, prayed to God, and inserted it into the padlock. I gently turned the key to the right, and a dry, clicking sound told me that the lock had opened. I lifted the lid of the box and withdrew the key. I smiled, then carefully pulled out the book that was inside, and turned to the first page, which read:

To Martin and Gail Thompson, from Auckland.

Departed New Zealand, this 3rd of March, 1998,

in "Distant Winds," for a trip of spiritual discovery

May your days be filled with happiness,

May your nights be filled with dreams;

May those dreams when you awake

bring you the magic that lies ahead.

May your dreams come true,

and later, become sweet memories.

And may you always remember...

Thomas Blake

I kept staring at the inscription, thinking back. It seemed like only yesterday that the old bookstore owner had given me this most treasured of gifts. "That was almost eight months ago," I thought.

How could we have imagined the parallel worlds we'd discover in the interim, the life challenges put in front of us? We'd have to stand against all the odds to defend what we believed in, and how close would all of it bring us once again?

It had been tough. But now, safe in port and with Gail asleep like an angel, I knew that we'd taken an extraordinary journey in life. A pilgrimage of re-discovery of ourselves, a real test that had saved our relationship and our love. We knew we needed to share an experience with others, those searching, like us, for the true meaning of life.

I gazed down at the key, absorbed in my own reflection. The face staring back at me seemed like the face of a completely different man. I now had brown hair and a pale, smooth complexion that contrasted sharply with my normal gray wisps of hair and mottled, wrinkled skin. Gone were the lines from stressful nights, gone were the wrinkles from squinting at tiny print in contracts and licenses. Could this person, with the likeness of an athletic twenty-year-old, actually be a middle-aged, pot-bellied man?

I slipped the key into my pocket, placed the book back in the box, and gently closed the lid. Our treasure was safe. We had plenty of time to spread the word. But now it was time to take care of Gail, my beloved wife. The woman I had once almost lost, personally and spiritually, but now re-discovered forever.

I

In my beautiful birthplace of New Zealand is Auckland, the largest city in an emerald green country, often referred to as "the land of the long cloud." Auckland itself is surrounded by lush green rolling hills. It is the majestic Bay of Auckland, where sailing boats arrive whispering tales of distant lands. Others depart in search of magic worlds.

***

As usual, I left home that morning, trying not to think about the pile of paperwork awaiting my "in" tray on my desk. It had been pouring all night, and on this soggy wet Monday morning, the traffic seemed worse than usual. After driving for almost an hour, I finally got to my building. I prepared myself for another week of tedious work.

I looked up at the dark building, which appeared to hunch ominously over me. I was forced to drive around boxes and pillars to reach my parking spot on the other side of the lot. It was the worst possible spot, stuck in a corner beside paint cans and brooms, even though I, working for next to nothing, generated most of the company's income.

I opened the car door and immediately stumbled over a board slung on the floor. God, I hated my job!

Still, a person can get used to anything, if given enough time to forget the true essence that lies within. There was a time when I believed anything was possible, and one day I'd conquer the world. Yet here I was, doing something that had nothing to do with the dreamer I was. Or had it been? Was it a rule that when one became a grown-up and faced the real world, we were bound to forget childhood reveries?

I walked across the parking lot to the stairs and began walking up to my office. The many turns on the spiraling staircase and the dim illumination of only occasional light bulbs didn't help alleviate my growing headache. When I reached my office, I opened the door and stepped inside.

I found myself in front of a tall pile of paperwork. I went through all the mail that had come late on Friday.

For some reason that defied all the physics laws, the harder I worked to clear the "in" tray, the higher the pile of paperwork got. I guess it was one of those things that happened to a busy person like me.

***

My office was on the eighteenth floor of a tall building overlooking the Bay of Auckland. I'd always considered it a mixed blessing having my office in this place. The ocean had always captivated me, and I could stare at the awesome view all day. But it sometimes felt as if I was spending my day in a golden cage, just watching the beauty around me pass by without enjoying it, or even being part of it. I had always had the traveler's bug. Although I had traveled around my country and Australia, I had been very busy with my work lately, spending long hours at the office. Not even having the time to leave Auckland during the weekend, since my wife's working schedule included most Saturdays and Sundays. Working hard was no offense, I thought, even though I still believed that I was wasting precious time perhaps meant for another purpose.

The office walls were painted a soft beige pastel, and on one hung an old map of the world. It always reminded me of all the places I knew existed. Places I had read about in travel magazines or watched portrayed on TV. Places I had always wished to see but had never gone to for one reason or another.

I had bought that map across the street in Mr. Blake's bookstore, an old shop just close to my building. I enjoyed browsing through the old books that seemed to stare at me from the shelves of his little but well-supplied shop. Every now and then, I would find a book that would catch my attention. I would buy it and take it home to read, sitting on the balcony of my apartment while watching the sun set in the deep blue ocean.

After having put the finishing touches on a contract, I decided to go to Blake's bookstore. But, on the way out, I ran into my new boss. He immediately began asking what I was doing, leaving so early. We had yet another heated argument. The man had arrived 10 days ago, and it seemed that he had brought with him an attitude of superiority. I sometimes felt like punching him. But this was the office and my financial future. I bit my lip, and dutifully turned around and went back to my desk, waiting for the last half hour.

The second my clock showed 8 p.m. I ran out the door and down the stairs. I walked across the street into Mr. Blake's world. As usual, I started browsing, hoping to discover some exciting titles.

A small book on the lower shelf caught my

attention:

"Step to the Music You Hear - Philosophical Poems from Modern and Classical Authors."

In it were poems and excerpts from different writers. I began reading one by one Henry David Thoreau, thoughts from "Walden Pond":

"Why should we be in such desperate haste to succeed and in such desperate enterprises? If a man does not keep pace with his companions, perhaps it is because he hears a different drummer. Let him step to the music which he hears, however measured or far away."

"Beautiful choice, Mr. Thompson," Mr. Blake said aloud. "Thoreau always had something to say to remind us of the importance of choosing our own destiny."

I stared at Mr. Blake, a short man with a long, gray beard parked behind an old pair of thick glasses and an old light-brown suit that showed its age. He then turned around and started to clean some books in one of the piles marked "on sale."

Mr. Blake had been working at the bookshop for as long as I could remember. And though the passage of time had stolen most of his sight, his memory was as brilliant as ever. He stared at the glass door that separated his small shop from the outside world.

"Turn to page nineteen, Mr. Thompson," he told me, "and you will find another great truth coming from our friend Thoreau."

I followed his instructions. Indeed, page nineteen contained another "Walden Pond" injunction:

"I went to the woods because I wished to live deliberately, to confront only the essential facts of life, and see if I could not learn what it had to teach, and not, when I came to die, discover that I had not lived."

Mr. Blake gazed at me. "Can you imagine that Henry David Thoreau was not always respected for his ideas when he was alive? Only after his death did people start to realize the stature of this man. He left society and everything he possessed and went into the woods for more than two years to discover the essential things in life. But isn't it always like this?"

"What do you mean?" I asked.

"Don't we almost always give more importance

to people who are already dead than those who are still alive? It is much easier to make a legend of someone we have only heard about but never known. Maybe because we don't see their human aspect we turn them into legends, without realizing that they were as human as you and I."

I smiled. "It is always a pleasure to listen to you, Mr. Blake. You wouldn't believe how good it feels after a long and tedious day at the office to come to your bookstore and just forget about it all."

"Well, it's good to hear that. Thank you, Mr. Thompson."

"I think I'll take the book," I said. I handed it to Mr. Blake, then started to walk towards the exit door, where an old cash register stood over a pile of dusty books.

"I'll give you this book at a special price Mr. Thompson. I think you will truly enjoy it."

"Well, thanks for that, Mr. Blake!" I took the money from my wallet and handed it to him. He operated the rusty cash register, which sounded as if it was on its last transaction.

"Thanks, Mr. Blake, and good-bye for now." I opened the front door of the shop and started to walk away.

"Why, Mr. Thompson?" I heard him ask.

I paused outside the shop, still holding the glass door, and turned back toward him.

"Why what?" I replied.

"Why does it feel so good to come here after work? Is it that you don't enjoy what you do during the day anymore?"

I stopped, still holding the door open. "Well, yes and no," I replied. "I can't complain about my job. I make some good money, and basically, I like it. It's just that sometimes I wonder if this is all I will ever do with my life. The routine makes me feel that I'd rather be doing something more rewarding, though not necessarily from a financial point of view. Something that could give more meaning to my existence and, at the same time, enrich my life and others' lives.

Every time I opened one of these books and realize all the different ways I could live, all those places that exist that I could go to. All the people I could meet, and all the things I could learn, wish I could take a break from my daily routine, and try to see the rest of the world. I don't know why, but sometimes I feel I'm missing something very important."

"So why don't you do it?" he asked.

"I have been able to save quite a bit of money that will help Gail and me a secure retirement, a good education for our children, and...".

"Turn to page forty-nine, Mr. Thompson."

"Excuse me?"

"Turn to page forty-nine of the book you just bought, please..."

I did what he said. I took the book from the paper bag, then open it on page forty-nine. There was another "Walden Pond" suggestion:

"If one advances confidently in the direction of his dreams, and endeavors to live the life he has imagined, he will meet with a success unexpected in common hours."

He smiled. "Your friend Thoreau does it again, Mr. Thompson."

I started feeling a little uncomfortable. It had been easy for me to think about these dreams as something far beyond my reach, something that belonged to my youth. Dreams that probably most people like me would love to realize but couldn't or wouldn't.

But I was faced with the fact that someone had

really done it and knowing from the way I was feeling and my tingling skin, I knew Mr. Blake and Thoreau had touched a heartstring. They made me realize that they had discovered something special that I knew existed but thought I could not reach. Maybe it wasn't so far beyond my reach as I had thought.

"Maybe you have been trying to find excuses for not doing what you know you have to do, Mr. Thompson. Maybe the time is now right", said Mr. Blake, putting on his glasses the way only booksellers do. "Anyway, I hope you enjoy the book." He turned back and went to help some other customers.

"Thanks, Mr. Blake." I put the book in the paper bag and placed it inside my coat pocket and walked toward my car. Time had sped past. Gail might be worrying about me. Or I hoped, even though our relationship had been on the rocks lately. Our jobs and busy schedules had pushed our bond into the background.

II

I wasn't prepared for the romantic scene that greeted me when I got home: a candle-lit table, a bottle of champagne on ice, steaming lasagna, and freshly cooked vegetables, a domestic feast.

"Happy fifth anniversary, Michael!" Gail said.

I couldn't conceal my surprise. Gail noticed it immediately.

"You didn't remember!" she shouted angrily. I noticed the pain in her eyes.

"I'm sorry, Gail, but I just can't do anything right these days. I can't think. I had another terrible day at work. I'm too tired to think straight, let alone…"

"And don't you think I also had a hard day at the office, only to rush home and prepare all this for you? At least I remembered our wedding anniversary!"

She ran upstairs, sobbing. I followed her.

"I'm sorry, love."

"Did you have another argument with your new boss?" she asked.

"Yes," I replied. "I just don't think we'll ever get

along, I have honestly tried, but God! The man is impossible. "

"Anything else?"

"No, why do you ask?"

"I know that look in your eyes."

"What look?" I asked.

"The one you have when you're thinking about something and looking for an answer."

She was right. Gail knew me well, one of the things I most admired about her. Her sensitive and beautiful green eyes saw into people and their thoughts.

We'd met in our last year of business school, and from the first moment, we'd been magnetically attracted to each other. It had lasted eight years, and I felt fortunate. My mother once told me that first love changes your life forever. It endures. No matter what you do, that feeling lingers until you die.

"You'll recognize it instantly," she told me, "because when you stare at her for the first time, everything surrounding her will fade away." That feeling, that blessing, that love, was a woman called Gail. She was strikingly beautiful, with brown hair, a pleasant smile, and olive skin. But it was her eyes, deep and green, that let you stare into the sweetness of her soul, that had stolen my heart.

She stopped crying, her sadness filling the whole room. "You know I am right here if you need me," she said.

"I know. Thanks for that."

But deep inside, I knew I was starting to lose her. This time her words sounded empty, so different from how she'd talked to me in our early years. The strong bond of our first years of marriage was withering in front of our eyes. We were at a loss on how to stop it. Somehow, our jobs and careers had kept us so busy and involved that we barely had time to see each other. Wasn't love enough for two persons to live happily forever?

I knew she was still trying hard to hide her tears and not to show her disappointment.

"It's a wonderful starry night," she said. "Why don't you go out to the porch, along with your thoughts?"

I knew she needed to be alone.

"Sure, love," I said.

I took my coat and went to the back porch, where

four brown chairs surrounde an old wooden-round table with the barbecue nearby. The night was fresh and crisp, and the sky was impregnated with thousands of tiny, brilliant lights. It had been a blessing to move away from the city to admire a night like this.

I remembered the book that I had bought. I decided to give it a quick look. I opened it randomly. There was a poem on page twenty-two:

Do what you want to do.

Be what you want to be.

Look the way you want to look.

Act the way you want to act.

Think the way you want to think.

Speak the way you want to speak.

Follow the goals

you want to follow.

Live according to the truths

within yourself.

"There goes Thoreau again," I thought to myself. This man had really discovered the real purpose of his life.

I was just about to turn the page when I saw the name of the author.

It wasn't Thoreau.

It was American poet Susan Polis Schulz.

Now I was feeling pretty puzzled. It wasn't only Thoreau who'd discovered his own truth; this woman had as well. How many more were there?

I started to feel uneasy. Who were these ghosts that had come inside an old book to challenge my way of life? I had always thought that I had been doing the right thing, making a living, and thinking about my own future and those I loved the most.

But now, the more I read about these strangers, the more I realized that they were not strangers to me. Some had lived their lives based on their own principles, without following pre-set rules, finding the truth of who they really were, and hence learned to live a more fulfilling life.

Gail came out to the porch. "Thought you may want a coffee."

"Thanks," I said. I took a small sip of the freshly

brewed coffee, as the brown liquid warmed me, as it gently slipped down my throat.

"Have a good night's sleep," said Gail, and started to walk towards the house.

"Gail?"

"Yes?"

"Would you stay with me for a while?"

"Hmm, OK." She sat at my side. "What are you reading?" she asked.

"Oh, just a small book I bought today in the bookstore close to work, the one owned by Mr. Blake. You remember Mr. Blake, don't you?"

"Hmm, not really," she said.

"You know, the old man we went to see once about a book from…"

"Oh, yes, I remember now. The man with the thick glasses."

"Exactly," I said.

She looked at the stars. "I remember seeing something special in that man."

"What do you mean?" I asked.

"Something in his eyes," Gail replied. "They glowed differently."

"What do you mean by that?" I pressed.

"I can't explain it. It's just one of those things I can detect in people. Anyway, it's not important." She turned towards me: "Can I see the book?"

"Sure. It's a book with very nice thoughts. You know, one of those books that you just open at any page and start reading."

She took the book from my hands, then slowly opened it without looking at the page number, and started reading:

"Though we travel the world over to find the beautiful, we must carry it with us or find it not."

"That's a wonderful truth," she said.

"Well, I just learned this morning about this guy called Thoreau. He is outstanding."

"It wasn't written by Thoreau," she said.

"What?"

"It wasn't written by Thoreau."

"Oh, yes, of course," I answered. "There is this great lady called Susan Polis Schulz that uses the same style and..."

"It wasn't written by her, either."

"Are you sure?"

"Of course, I'm sure," she said. "Here it says that it was written by Ralph Waldo Emerson."

I kept silent. I just kept staring at the open book, thinking.

"Are you okay, Michael?"

"Sure, Gail, I'm okay. I'm just thinking."

She stared at me. "Well then, I'll leave you alone with your thoughts," she said. "But don't take too long. We have to get up early. I have a very long day at work tomorrow."

"Won't we have dinner, Gail?"

"I lost my appetite, Michael. I want to go to sleep."

"OK," I answered. "Good night."

"Good night, Michael." She then stood up and left.

I kept staring at the open book. I was starting to feel uncomfortable, and the chair that felt so good before now felt like a cold, hard piece of stone. Who were these people? How could they have written about the same issues? Did they know each other? Of course not! At least not all of them. But if they had come from different walks of life, how could they feel the same way, and transmit the same message?

Why did I feel so close to their thoughts, and at the same time, so far from their lives? Would I ever have the courage to follow their steps to discover the truth they had found?

And then, a thought hit me like lightning, and made me feel even worse:

How many more people in the world were living the life they were supposed to live, having already taken the tough decision of following their hearts?

I closed the book, frightened. I now knew there were many more than I had ever expected.

III

The next morning, I left home late for work, knowing that I would inevitably be caught in the morning traffic.

I hadn't been able to sleep the night before and spent quite a bit of time reading the book I had purchased at Blake's bookstore. I discovered poems written by people such as Ella Wheeler Wilcox, Douglas Malloch, Robert Pollis, and others. They realized they all had one thing in common: they had lived their lives based on their own principles. They had listened to the voice within themselves and put into practice what they had preached. They had given meaning to their lives.

How had they done it? Had someone helped them? Were they so strong and I so weak that I couldn't imagine ever being like them, even though at this moment I wished it more than anything in my life?

***

The day nearly went by without me noticing it.

Sometimes work at the office was so standardized that I could do it without really concentrating. I left the office in a daze but ran into the Chairman on the stairs. He made an observation of the way I was dressed, saying it was inappropriate for the workplace. There was nothing wrong with a suit, now, was there? The issue appeared to be the dark green shirt. Was this man's sole purpose in life to make my life miserable? I kept mumbling yes sir, of course, sir, won't happen again, sir, and finally was able to leave. I went into my car and headed home. Almost without noticing it, another day had passed me by.

That night I kept staring at the book again. I was feeling pretty bad about myself. Gail noticed it immediately, and although she was still angry with me, she quietly came to my side.

"Still thinking about the answers to your thoughts?" she asked. "Don't forget, I'm a good listener." She stared at me with that look full of love, trying to find a way to open the door that separated us. We knew that the other was there, behind that wall we had built, which made us feel so far away from each other.

"I need to tell you something, Gail."

"What is it?" she asked.

I felt a tear rolling down my cheek. "Remember the book I bought yesterday?"

"Yes."

"Well, I finished reading it last night and stayed up all night thinking about the people who had written all those wonderful poems. I really envy them, you know?"

"Why?" she asked.

"Because I would love to be like them. To live my life based on what I believe in, without worrying so much about our future. Without worrying so much about what others would think about me."

"So why don't you do it?"

"I guess it´s the life that we are living, love. The daily routine, the thought of a safe financial future now that our careers are going well has made me lose some of that spirit of adventure I always had."

"Then recapture it, Michael. Bring it back. Be a free spirit again."

"Gail, you know that we've spent a lot of time and effort building a financial nest that will let us have a peaceful retirement and have the means to start a family and give our kids the best in life. Isn't that the reason we work so hard? We can't just throw all that effort away. If we quit our jobs to follow some crazy dream, we'll lose some of the financial benefits we have worked so hard to achieve."

She looked at me. Her look was strong and determined.

"Michael Thompson, listen to me and listen well. I married you because I knew that someday we would have a chance to live a special life, a life in which nothing would hold us back. Remember the free spirits we were when we met for the first time? I fell in love with that special light you had in your eyes, and I knew someday that something would happen that would help us build our own Heaven on Earth. Maybe the time is now."

"Time for what?" I asked.

"Time to make a radical change in our lives. Love, I didn't want to tell this to you before, but I have to. I see the sadness you are feeling. I can tell you that I have been feeling the same emptiness you are experiencing as if there was no purpose or meaning in the things we are doing. Sometimes I don't recognize myself, Michael, putting so much emphasis on my career and my financial future at the expense of my time and personal life, and I am becoming someone I know I don't want to be. We barely see each other, we don't talk like we used to do, and I'm starting to feel like a stranger around you. If you feel the same way, why don't we recover our spirit of adventure, and become the true lovers we once were? What can go wrong? We are still dreamers, and we love each other. The worst that can happen is that if we don't feel better with our new way of life we can always return to our old lifestyle, find new jobs, and save less money than we hoped. That's all we can lose. On the other hand, can you imagine all the wonderful places we can discover, the different people we can meet, and all the things we can learn from them?"

"We only live once, Michael, and if life passes us by, there is no turning back. Don't you think that when we get older, we will regret not having given our dream a chance?"

"Yes, Gail, but..."

Without noticing, I dropped the book from the table. It fell to the floor and opened on page twelve.

A journey of a thousand miles

Starts with the first step...

in the right direction.

We stared at the open book in silence. Gail smiled, then started laughing, and looked at me. "I think your friends are trying to tell you something, love."

"We only live once," Gail had said. I looked at the open book on the floor, and then, for the first time in a long while, I knew the answer had been given. Gail was right. These were no strangers coming to me through an old book. These were people as human as me who had discovered the secret of living a fulfilling life. That now had come to help me take the first steps towards the life I had always dreamt of having. And now I finally realized that if I followed my heart and made my own decisions, these soul-mates would be there to help me and guide me.

I took Gail's hand and looked her in the eye.

"Gail?"

"Yes, love?"

My hands were trembling.

"Gail, if something doesn't work out well, if we suffer while trying to follow our dreams, if someday we're not able to have the things that we once wanted so badly, will you still love me?"

She looked straight into my heart, tears rolling

from her beautiful green-emerald eyes.

"I have loved you all my life, Michael. And before knowing you, I had loved the thought of you. And before that, I had loved the promise of someone like you. No matter whatever happens to us, Michael Thompson, I will love you forever."

I was speechless. I didn't know what to say now that Gail had said it all. I had promised her these adventures, these dreams so many times before, but I had never delivered the goods. Action and not only ideas are what make dreams come true. And now, I knew she was begging me not to disappoint her once more because maybe this would be the last chance to save our relationship, our marriage.

I was keenly aware of the effect my answer would have for the rest of our lives. So, I just said the first thing that came to my mind.

"Gail, do you remember that dream we had about buying a sailing boat and going on a trip..."

I couldn't finish. Gail rushed towards me, her eyes full of tears, and hugged me with all her strength.

"I love you, Michael Thompson," she said.

IV

We waited until the end of the week to start searching for a boat.

Although we were good sailors, Gail and I had never owned a boat. We had sailed around the Bay of Auckland in large and small vessels with friends and ourselves. Still, we had never ventured outside the Bay, not because we didn't want to, but because we never seemed to find the time to do it.

We approached a small marina with a colorful sign hanging at the end of the pier, which read "BOATS FOR SALE." A flight of old rusty stairs led to an office at the end of the dock. We opened the door, and a tinkle of music let the owner know that prospective customers had arrived.

"Welcome to the best boat shop in town!" said a short young fellow with dark eyes and wearing a suit that could only be that of a salesman. "My name is John Roberts. How can I help you this morning?"

"Well, Mr. Roberts," I said, "my name is Michael, and this is my wife Gail, and we want to buy a sailboat. To tell you the truth, we've never owned a boat before, so we would appreciate your suggestions and advice."

"Well, you've come to the right place!" he said. "By the way, please call me John." He brought out a catalog of old and new boats for sale. "What kind of trip are you planning to make?" he asked.

"We are planning to sail out of Auckland and probably go all the way to Fiji and Vanuatu before returning home through New Caledonia."

His eyes opened in disbelief. "Are you telling me you want to make such a trip, and you have never owned a sailing boat?"

"Well, yes and no," answered Gail. "We have never had a boat of our own, but we have quite a bit of experience sailing around Auckland, and we feel it is time to make a longer trip."

Mr. Roberts started to perspire. He pulled out a white handkerchief from the back pocket of his trousers and started to wipe his forehead.

"Well, this is going to be a tricky one, if you want to go bareboat," he said.

"What do you mean by bareboat?" I asked, without understanding.

"Bareboat is a term used in sailing to describe a trip in which you don't use a professional crew. That means that you will probably have to be the skipper, Michael, and your wife, the crew. It's not impossible to handle, but it is very important to choose the right boat and the right equipment. In your case, we'll have to look for a boat with the three most important features for serious sailing: a good hull, a good rig, and a reliable engine." He stood up. "Let me show you what I've got," he said.

He took us to the luxury-deluxe end of his sailboat fleet: boats with all the latest cruising devices, such as roller furling headsails; roller furling mainsails, sonar systems, satellite navigation, solar power systems; and all possible luxuries such as walk-through transoms with dive platforms, *bimini*, which is the name given to areas of the boat with permanent shade; cockpit table with icebox; stern showers; stack quadraphonic CD sound systems, microwave and all the unimaginable luxuries a modern sailboat could offer.

We stared at the boats like children, trying to take in all Mr. Roberts was telling us. We weren't happy as it wasn't luxury what we were looking for, but safety.

He stared at us. "Well, don't panic," he said. "I'll show you the boats I call, in general, standard." He took us towards a group of white sailing boats anchored at the right side of the pier. "Please take your time," he said. "Most of these boats will be able to take you on your trip, with only small adjustments."

We started browsing. Brands such as Catalinas, Beneataus, and Hunters appeared here and there. All the boats were different, but they all seemed safe and at reasonable conditions. However, no matter how many times we would get in and out of the boats, something was missing. For some reason that I couldn't pinpoint, something wasn't right. I knew Gail felt the same way.

We spent the next three hours comparing designs, prices, and configurations. Details such as stability and maneuverability were taken into account and compared between boats. Safety was mentioned, again and again, stressing that we would find ourselves out in the sea without touching land for several days at a time.

We couldn't decide what to do. Something was not quite right. Although some of the boats mentioned by Mr. Roberts sounded impeccable, we didn't feel totally at ease with sailing in them.

Mr. Roberts was about to give up. Realizing that he would not make a sale that morning, he gave us his card and told us to come back once we had made up our minds.

"Think about it," he said, trying to hide his frustration. "I'm not going anywhere."

We left the pier, our heads down, wondering if

we were trying to play a game that only experts could. "Don't worry, love," I said to Gail. "Better to take our time than to make a mistake."

"You're right," said Gail. "Maybe we should re-think all this crazy idea and..."

She suddenly stopped. Her eyes stared behind the boat shop. There was an old sailing boat, chained to the wall, with a "for sale" sign hanging on its side. The wood of the ship was part rotten, and the sail had holes in some places. I had to strain to see the boat as it was anchored in a dark, isolated area. I looked back at Gail and began wondering if she had temporarily lost her sanity.

"Gail, are you okay?"

She kept staring at the boat for several minutes without talking. Then suddenly she turned back and started running towards Mr. Roberts' office. He saw her approaching and came out of the door.

"Is there anything wrong, Madame?"

"Mr. Roberts, that boat for sale, the one behind the boathouse, is it yours?"

"Well, yes," he said. "But that boat won't take you far. It's very old and can only be used around the Bay."

I stared at Gail.

"Gail, what are you doing?"

She didn't answer me.

"Mr. Roberts, do you think you could fix it so we could use it for our trip?"

He stared at the boat. "Hmm, I guess we could, but it would cost a lot of money."

"How much?"

"That depends on what you want."

"It has to be in good enough shape to take us where we want to go," Gail said.

"It will take some time to calculate how much it will cost," said Mr. Roberts.

"Well then," said Gail, "let's go back to your office and make us an offer with the boat ready to sail, including all basic equipment."

"This will take some time," he said.

"Never mind," said Gail. "It's taken a long time for me to start dreaming again. A couple of hours won't hurt. I still have the rest of my life."

Mr. Roberts went inside his private office and brought out manuals about nautical devices, radio equipment, structure, and others. He was now sweating so much that I had to lend him my own handkerchief.

"Thank you," he said, going back immediately to his computer, typing in numbers, adding, subtracting, checking his manuals.

I spoke to Gail very quietly.

"Gail, what are you doing?"

She stared at me. "I am doing something I should have done a long time ago."

"And what is that?" I asked.

"I am following my instinct," she said.

Finally, the printer started to work, sending a long piece of paper with a final sum at the end. Mr. Roberts took it, checked the list for the last time, and then wrote a number on the back of the paper.

He looked straight at us. "Michael, Gail, you have really made me work hard today. I've already taken ten percent off the original price, so don't even try to bargain. This is my final offer: take it or leave it. I can guarantee you that with all this navigational equipment, and repairs to the hull, you will be safe to make your trip in this old sailing boat." He gently slipped the piece of paper to our side of the table. "Now I will leave you guys alone, so you can make a decision." He quietly left the room.

We saw the price. We stared at each other.

"Gail, there is no way we could pay such a price!"

"Michael, you know we can, we'll just have to use the money for our retirement."

"What? We can't touch that money, you know that!"

"We've come this far, we have to, and anyway, you know we can."

And just for an instant, I felt what Gail was feeling. She was right. Of course, we could use that money. It was our money. Saving it for a time still far away was a way to find an excuse to continue living the stressful life we were living and hated so much. Still, it was inbred in us to not touch it for "security."

What would be better? To keep the money and have a safe and quiet retirement, or to embark on a beautiful adventure that would make us feel we had accomplished a fully lived life?

Even more, we could always return and sell the boat at the end of the trip, and in this way, recover most of our initial investment. The memories, however, would last an eternity. They would be priceless. It could even be the way to get close to each other again. We had nothing to lose, now that our marriage was falling to pieces.

It was an argument too strong not to be taken into account.

We stared at each other. "You already know the decision," I said.

"Yes!" Gail. She stood up and went outside the office.

"Mr. Roberts, you have a deal."

He gave us a big smile. "I'll start working on the boat immediately. It'll be ready in two weeks."

"That's perfect," I said. We shook hands and signed a check for half the price of the boat. The other half would be paid once the ship was fully renovated.

Mr. Roberts walked with us to where our "new" sailing boat was anchored. It looked really old. Yet there was something special about it, and I began to understand what Gail had noticed before.

"What's she called?" I asked.

"I really don't know," Mr. Roberts answered.

"Her nameplate probably fell off some time ago. You know, old boats".

"Don't you have any records of the previous owner?" I asked.

"Yes, I do," Mr. Roberts said. "But for some odd reason, the name of the boat is never mentioned. The model, the color, the engine number, and registration are, but not the name. It was registered as a Catalina sailing boat. But believe me, it's not important; all the papers are in order. Besides, maybe it's a good chance for you to give it your own name, don't you think?" he added.

***

We stayed at the marina until well after the sun had set.

We sat on the bench just in front of the boat staring at it for hours on end, the same way children do when they get that special present they dream of. We were a bit scared and not too sure about what we had done. But we had also learned that this is the way you feel when a significant change comes into your life. When you are about to leave what Gail and I called "the safety zone," that place in your personal world becomes a routine, and you feel safe because everything is familiar. When all that is about to change, you suddenly feel a little out of place.

"What will we name her?"

"What?"

"What will we name her?" Gail asked again.

"Well, I'm not sure," I answered. "Any ideas?"

"Hmm, not right now," she said.

"Well, then I guess it's better to leave it for another day." I stood up. "Let's go home, Gail. It's getting late."

"I don't want to go," she said. "I'm afraid that if we leave now, the magic of our dream will be broken, and we will start having second thoughts."

Gail looked beautiful when she was worried. You could see her green eyes speaking with the truth of her heart. She had never learned to lie, and that was one of the things I loved most about her, one of the things I was so desperately trying to bring back to our relationship.

"Don't worry," I said. "The boat will still be here tomorrow, and if we've come this far, I don't think we'll have second thoughts."

She looked at me. "Okay, I trust you," she said. I grabbed her hand, and we slowly walked towards the car. And then I realized I couldn't remember how long it had been since the last time we had walked together holding hands when our silence was more important than any words we could speak.

***

That night we started making all the arrangements to leave in two weeks on our new and nameless boat.

Though it was not a new boat, it was in reasonably good condition. Mr. Roberts explained that the last owner had done an excellent job by not letting the propellers rust, and the small engine still worked like a clock. The hull looked worse than it really was, and the condition of our boat was, in general, pretty good. Mr. Roberts assured us it was a very sailable boat. With extras such as a CD sound system, gas stove, oven, top quality dinnerware, stainless steel cookware, and shower, it would be even more enjoyable. A new radio system based on satellite detection would be installed for communication purposes and to ensure our safety.

I looked at Gail, and she smiled back at me.

How could we have imagined how far away from the truth we were at that moment, thinking about all those material comforts when we were about to discover the real treasures of life?

V

Two weeks had passed since we purchased the sailing boat when we received a call from Mr. Roberts, telling us that it was ready. We had rushed to the marina. In the beginning, we could barely recognize our boat. It had a new paint job, and the bright white didn't manage to divert our attention from the gleaming polished deck. The smell of freshly ground cedar and new sails added to the enchantment. The stove and fridge looked starkly new against the primitive but spotless farm-style table. We now knew we would spend many hours of the day, cooking and sampling so many foreign foods that somehow would link us to their own unique cultures. Mr. Roberts had added all the extras he had mentioned and replaced most of the stern and all navigational equipment. It looked brand new, as well as safe. The forty-five-foot schooner looked majestic.

We paid Mr. Roberts the money we owed him, and he gave us all the documents that said that the boat now belonged to us. "I hope you have a wonderful trip, Gail and Michael. And don't forget that on your return, I would be interested in buying back your boat."

"Thanks, John, for the offer," I replied. "We'll see when we come back."

We shook hands and then left. Gail was carrying with her the most beautiful smile in the world.

***

I went to the office the next morning. Since it was my last day of work, I said good-bye to my colleagues. They had been great with me after giving them the news of my departure from the company. Although most of them couldn't understand why I was doing what I was doing, they all wished me well. We had a couple of drinks together. Then, after lunch, I said goodbye to my peers, and then to my boss, even though I expected him to begin arguing with me about my decision. To my pleasant surprise, he did nothing of the kind.

"We're going to miss you," he said, and for an instant felt a sense of envy coming through his eyes.

I was awestruck, but now surer then ever about the course we had taken.

I started walking towards my car. I opened the door and was about to start the engine when a thought came to me.

Mr. Blake.

I had to say good-bye to Mr. Blake, as well as tell him the news.

I didn't know how long it would be before my return. As I usually visited Blake's bookstore twice a week, it would be better to tell him that I was leaving for a while, so he wouldn't worry about me. Anyway, he would probably congratulate me. "I hope the bookstore is still open," I thought.

I got out of the car and walked across the street as I had done so many times. The bookstore was still open, and Mr. Blake was sitting at the end of the aisle, reading.

"Mr. Blake!"

"Hello, my friend," he said. He stood up and approached me. "How are you doing today?" he asked.

"Very well, Mr. Blake. I just came by to say good-bye."

"Are you leaving town?" he asked.

"Well, yes," I answered. "My wife and I are going on a trip in our new sailing boat, and we don't know how long the trip will take. I came by to say goodbye, so you wouldn't worry if you didn't see me soon."

"Very thoughtful of you," Mr. Thompson. He smiled at me. "So, you did it."

"Did what?" I asked.

"You've quit your job, and you will follow your dream."

"Well, I guess so," I said, "At least for a while. I need to find a purpose in what I am doing; I need to find out who I really am."

"Do you know what our friend Samuel Butler said?"

"Who?"

"Samuel Butler, someone like those you've been reading about. "Life is like music. It must be composed by ear, feeling, and instinct, not by rule." He walked to the back aisle, sat on a chair, and opened a wooden drawer. He pulled out a package covered with plain gift-wrapping. The box was about the size of a large book.

"This is for you and your wife," he said.

"Mr. Blake, you shouldn't have..." Then it hit me. "How did you know that I was leaving?"

He smiled. "I knew it from the very first moment," he said. "I knew you had the strength to follow your heart."

He handed me the package. I started to open it.

"No, wait!" he said and held my hands. "Please don't open it yet."

"What do you mean?" I asked, without understanding.

"Don't open it until you have set sail. You must do so. Do it as a favor to an old man that has very old habits. Who knows, it might bring you some good luck."

I was a little skeptical. "Well, if you want it that way..."

"Yes, Mr. Thompson, thank you. Do not open it until you have left the pier, and you have started your journey."

I nodded my head in sign of approval; I took the gift and gave Mr. Blake a firm handshake. He came to me and hugged me.

"Bye for now," I said.

"Bye for now," he replied. I was just leaving the shop when he called me back.

"Mr. Thompson..."

"Yes,"

"One more thing. Once you have opened your present, please promise me that you will keep it until the end of the journey, no matter how absurd this may seem."

"Mr. Blake, you're starting to scare me."

"Don't be scared. I apologize if I am causing you any distress. Do it for an old man...."

I was getting grumpy. "Okay, I won't open it until I leave port, and I will keep it for the length of the journey."

"Thanks, Mr. Thompson." He stared at me, took his thick old glasses off, and with a beautiful smile said:

"Have a wonderful life, Michael."

He then turned and went back to his world of books, to where he belonged.

I didn't say anything. I just pushed the door open and left the bookstore. There were many things to do before leaving.

***

The sun was gradually disappearing over the horizon, leaving the sky a luminescent orange. The bright, blue water reflected the sunlight, and the wisps of clouds overhead completed the picture. Sudden warmth infused my soul. It was beautiful and helped convince me we should continue with this journey.

Gail and I sipped a cup of coffee aboard our boat, looking at each other and at sea. We had finished planning everything and had decided to spend the night in the boat, a night filled with the smell of the sea, ready to depart first thing in the morning.

After the romantic dusk, spots of light glittered and twinkled before my eyes. The stars were brighter than I had ever seen, and I was filled with awe at this clean and unpolluted environment.

"I'm so glad we've made this decision," Gail said. "I am already starting to feel better, just sitting here on the upper deck of our boat, closer to my true self, learning to live another kind of life, the free spirit I once was. Can you imagine how long we will be without following schedules, routines, or deadlines? We can do what we want, stop where we want, for as long as we want. God, I feel so young!" She looked at me. "Michael, are you listening to me?"

"I'm sorry, love," I said.

"Gail?"

"Yes, love?"

"Gail, did I tell you that Mr. Blake gave us a present for our trip?"

"No, you didn't. What is it?"

"I don't know. It was kind of weird. He asked me not to open it until we were at sea and made me promise that no matter what we thought about it, that we should keep it until the end of the journey."

"Well, she said, you know bookstore owners. They're kind of eccentric, and Mr. Blake is also an old man." She stared at me. "Where is it?"

"Down in the cabin," I said.

"Well, bring it, and let's open it."

"He said not to open it until we were in the ocean."

"Aren't you curious?"

"I just think we should respect the old man's wishes. He did sell me the book that started this."

"Yes, but technically we are at sea," Gail said. "We won't go back to dry land, and we are not at the pier. We are at the side of the pier, in our boat, on the ocean."

"All right, you're still as feisty as ever." I smiled. "Okay, I will bring it." I went into the cabin, opened the cupboard, and took the package. I went back to the upper deck, sat down, and gave it to Gail.

"You open it," I said.

"Why me?"

"It was your idea," I replied. "Besides, if it contains a curse or some other kind of spell, it will stick to you."

"You coward!" she said, laughing. She gently removed the wrapping paper to uncover a small wooden box with a lock. The key was also there.

"Should we open it?" I asked.

"Of course," she said, laughing. "That's what locks are for'!" She turned the key. The lock opened, and she lifted up the lid.

"What is it?" I asked.

She placed her hand inside the box and took out what was there.

"It's a book," she said.

"Hmm, it looks very old to me," I said.

She gently opened it. There was something written on the first page:

To Martin and Gail Thompson, from Auckland.

Departed New Zealand,

This 3rd of March 1997, in "Distant Winds,"

for a trip of spiritual discovery

May your days be filled with happiness,

May your nights be filled with dreams;

May those dreams when you awake

bring you the magic that lies ahead.

May your dreams become true,

and later, sweet memories.

And may you always remember...

Thomas Blake

We stared at each other.

"How did he know that we were leaving?"

"I don't know," said Gail. "Did you tell him?"

"No, I didn't. I went to his shop to tell him that I would be leaving for a while and to say good-bye. He had the gift already wrapped when I got there."

"Hmm, that's strange," Gail said. "Let's see what else it says." She started turning the pages, one by one. She began to turn them faster and faster.

"This is weird!" Gail said.

"What is it?" I asked.

"Besides what Mr. Blake wrote on the first page, this book is blank, empty. There is nothing else written. It is full of blank, empty pages."

"That's impossible," I said.

I took the book and checked it page by page.

She was right. They were all blank pages.

"Why would he do something like that?" I said.

"I don't know," answered Gail. "Did he tell you anything else?"

"Well, yes. To make sure we kept the book until the end of the trip."

"Well, now this is getting really weird," Gail said.

"What should we do?" I asked.

We kept silent for a while, thinking.

Gail was the first to speak.

"I think we should keep it. That Mr. Blake has a special glow in his eyes, and unless he is totally senile, which I don't think, he wouldn't have given us this present for no reason."

"Well, if you want it that way, that's fine by me. There won't be any harm done in keeping it until the end of the trip anyway. Besides, maybe we can use it as a diary."

Then I remembered something else.

"Gail?"

"What?"

"Can you read that first paragraph again?"

"Sure." She opened the book to the first page.

"To Martin and Gail Thompson, from Auckland.

Departed New Zealand,

This 3rd of March 1997, in "Distant Winds,"

For a trip of spiritual discovery..."

I stared at her. "How did he know the exact date when we were going to leave?"

She stared at me, smiling.

"Remember that our boat still doesn't have a name?"

We stared at each other, in total amazement, not knowing what to think.

Then Gail looked at the horizon, her golden hair flying with the evening breeze. A smile came to her.

"Distant Winds," she whispered. "I love it."

VI

Timing is essential when making decisions that will change the destiny of one's life.

It is not only doing the right thing that will take us to a safe port. It is equally important to do it at the right time. Everything has its own, precise moment in life, and if we want to rush it, it won't work. However, we must be alerted to ensure that the right moment doesn't pass us by, as sometimes that moment might never come back to give us a second chance.

That morning we set the sails of "Distant Winds" towards the horizon. Our hearts were beating fast, the wind blowing in our faces and adrenaline rushing through our veins, as the gray and white seagulls of Auckland escorted us out of the bay. We had been waiting for this moment to come true. We had placed so much effort into an endeavor. The time finally comes to start to live the dream.

In the beginning, we cannot believe it is really happening. It takes some time for the truth to settle in our minds. When we finally realize we have started to live our dream, an incredible feeling of accomplishment follows. It makes one feel a little unique, different from the rest. The dream finally starts to turn into reality.

***

After sailing for an hour, we lost sight of Auckland. We had decided to sail northeast, heading towards the Kermadec Islands, a group of volcanic Islands that were part of the New Zealand dependencies, 600 miles from Auckland. It was the first time we had been by ourselves without seeing dry land. The feeling of being alone, although good, also gave us a bit of apprehension.

"Gail?"

"Yes, love?"

"I guess this is going to sound a bit stupid, but you know, this is our last chance to quit this trip and go back to port. Maybe this is a crazy idea for a pair of grown-ups." I saw her face. I knew she was experiencing the same anguish I was. Although she was trying to tell me that everything would be okay, that we had the best equipment, that nothing terrible would happen. But she knew in her heart, just as I did, that indeed something could go wrong. And although our relationship had started to turn for the better, we still could feel that distance between our souls, which kept us from trusting each other completely.

"We have worked very hard on this project, Gail, but maybe you are right. Maybe we should re-think the whole thing and return to..."

Suddenly, a gentle breeze of wind from the west hit the bow of "Distant Winds," opening the book that Mr. Blake had given us. To our surprise, there was something written:

Don't be afraid

of the vastness of the Universe,

because you will find your place in it.

Thomas Blake

We stared at each other. "You told me there was nothing written in this book!" Gail said. "Didn't you check it well?"

"Gail, you checked it yourself. I swear there was nothing written, besides the first page. Look, it's the second page. It would have been impossible to miss it unless it was glued together."

"But if it was glued together, then how come it's

unglued now?"

We were silent. Gail took my hands and placed them on her face. "Michael, something strange and wonderful is happening, and although I am a little scared, I know that we have to believe in this dream."

"I know," I said. I took the book and closed it. I was about to put it back in the box when Gail stopped me.

"Leave it outside, at least while the weather is good."

"Are you sure?" I asked.

"Yes, love. I've got a hunch."

I didn't say anything. When Gail had a hunch, it was better to follow it.

VII

A week went on by, a week in which we learned many things about sailing.

We had started to familiarize ourselves with the winds that blew in this region of the world. As we sailed away from the New Zealand coast, we began feeling the southerly winds from the Antarctic that often blew at this time of the year. It would be safer to head north towards warmer waters. The winds coming from the South Pole were already starting to hit the southern island of New Zealand, making the seas treacherous for sailing. We had been informed of very gusty winds, up to forty knots, and rough seas south off Cook's Strait, which separates the two main islands of New Zealand.

If everything went well, we would arrive at the Kermadec Islands no later than March 17th, well before the southerly winds would reach that region. We were averaging 100 miles per day. This would give us plenty of time to get used to "Distant Winds" while the weather was mild, and we were still not far away from the New Zealand coast and its dependencies. Besides, Mr. Roberts had installed a state-of-the-art radio transmitter that worked with satellites, which we use to inform the local Coast

Guards of our daily position. It made us feel much safer, especially during the first days of our trip.

We had learned that we could sail faster and safer in the afternoons, as the warm winds that traditionally came from the west would turn cooler and shift southwest. This gentle breeze would place "Distant Winds" on course, saving us from moving the sails as often as we had to do it during the mornings.

To do this, we had to change some of our habits. We would have lunch earlier than we usually did. This way, we had plenty of time to rest and be ready to handle the sails for the full afternoon, possibly well into the night. We would have some fun cooking or fishing during the morning, waiting for the winds to shift. It was easy to recognize this change. You could feel an abrupt decline in temperature that gently cooled "Distant Winds" and us from the intense midday sun.

This simple experience of changing our eating habits made us realize that most of our routines back home had been made for convenience. Although we knew there was nothing wrong with them, that's all they were: routines and how they could be changed or even avoided. Having lunch at work at eleven in the morning would have been considered unusual. Here it wasn't. Without noticing it, we had started to see things differently, from another perspective. In the freedom and solitude that surrounded us, there were no rules. Everything was possible because here, we indeed had the main ingredient needed for a real change to take place: time.

***

One afternoon we set our sails as usual once the wind had changed. We had a very light breeze, so it was best to let the jib, the front sail, loosen up a bit, as this was the best way to handle soft winds. We had started to learn how to put the right curvature of the sail by trial and error, tightening and loosening the winch that operated the mainsail tightness. It seemed to get easier the more we practiced.

But this time, something went terribly wrong. We had finished setting up the sail, in the perfect position to use the soft wind. All of a sudden, a gust of wind came from the opposite direction, breaking the knot and sending the sail spinning. I threw myself overboard to dodge it, and from the water, as if in slow motion, I could see it going for Gail.

"Gail, watch out!" I shouted.

It was too late. She tried her best to avoid it but to no avail. An audible thump was heard when the pole hit her on the arm.

I climbed back up, secured the sails, and then rushed to her side.

"Are you okay, Gail?"

I could see her containing the tears. "I'm fine," she said. "I don't think it's broken."

"Just wait here, and don't move your arm. I'll bring the first aid kit."

I rushed into the cabin and started looking for the box. I could see everything but the first aid kit. I frantically started looking for it, as I heard Gail sobbing quietly on the upper deck. "It must hurt her a lot," I thought. I finally found it and went to her side. She was trembling, as now the shock of the pain was filtering through her.

I gently started checking the bones to see if there was any damage. "This is going to hurt a little," I said. She bravely handled the pain. Fortunately, there were no broken bones, but the lower part of her arm was starting to look like the rainbow's colors. I gently rubbed her arm with a soothing cream and carefully started wrapping it with an elastic bandage. After a few minutes, I finished, and gently placed the arm into a sling I made with a triangular bandage to immobilize it.

"Good!" I said. I looked at her, then gave her a soft kiss." You'll be like new in a couple of days."

"I feel awful," she said. "I won't be able to help you. I feel useless."

"Don't say that," I replied. "You will do the things you can, and we'll take it easy for the next few days."

"I don't want to be a burden," said Gail. "I was hoping this journey would help bring us together, but now this!" She then sat down, shook her head, and started crying. The emotional pain made the physical pain seem even worse.

I was about to tell her not to worry, when that wind that I was now starting to recognize so well came again, opening the book:

What will those who complain about life

say about death?

Thomas Blake

Gail looked at me, scared. "What is he trying to say? She asked.

"Well, love, I guess our good friend is trying to remind you that you should try not to complain about the pain you feel since you're still alive. Because if you weren't able to feel this pain, you wouldn't be able to feel happiness, love, or all the other beautiful things in life."

She stared at the horizon, her green eyes looking into her own soul. "You're right," she said, wiping the tears from her face. "That pole could have hit me harder, and who knows what could have happened. I shouldn't be complaining about it. I should be happy that nothing worse happened to me and that nothing happened to you. This is just a small accident that won't spoil our dream."

I smiled. "I guess you got the idea," I said.

Suddenly the book turned to the next page. We looked at it. The page was empty.

"There must be a mistake," I said. I gently closed the book.

The wind came back and opened it to the same blank page.

"I'd better take it back to the cabin," I said. I was about to take it when Gail held my hand.

"No!" she said. "Leave it as it is." She was experiencing something I couldn't perceive. I kept silent, waiting for her next move.

She stared at the horizon, and her voice sounded like a whisper in the cool breeze: "Never lose sight of the big picture. Never lose sight of what you first went on to achieve."

"That's beautiful, Gail," I said. "Where did you learn it?"

"I just made it up," she said, smiling.

"Well, you should have been a poet," I said. I stood up." Now it's time for you to rest. I'll clean everything and then go downstairs."

"Thanks, love, she said." She started walking downstairs.

"Gail, stop!"

She looked at me. "What's wrong?"

"Come and look for yourself!"

She came to my side, and we both stared at the page that had been blank before:

Never lose sight

of the big picture.

Never lose sight

of what

you first went on

to achieve.

Gail

We kept silent for a while, staring at each other. And just for an instant, I caught a glimpse of pure love coming from her soul through her eyes; that love I had missed so much and was now desperately trying to win back.

"What do you reckon?" she asked.

I smiled.

"I guess we're starting to remember who you and I are, Gail, who we are."

VIII

Lighthouses always guide sailors, even in the darkest of nights.

We learned this lesson when arriving late one night at the Kermadec Islands. We had preferred not to go into the inner bay until the sun had risen. We were still not too familiar with the navigational charts we were using. Still, the fact that we could see a beam of light coming from the lighthouse made us feel more secure, safer as if its light would hold "Distant Winds" position throughout the night.

We had had some rough days at sea. The southerly winds were moving northwards. But "Distant Winds" had turned into an indomitable sailing boat that would navigate as smooth as the dolphins that accompanied us through the high seas. Additionally, Gail's injuries had healed completely, and we were both becoming good sailors.

We felt astonished the next morning when we first saw the vast volcanic mountains of Sunday Island, the largest of the Kermadecs. Sunday Island was the only inhabited island, with a meteorological station installed some years ago. The magic of these pristine islands overwhelmed us, and we were filled with awe at the green, perfect picture of nature. A lush green blanket covered the island, ending only at the steep cliffs. Hundreds of migratory birds swooped and soared around and over the islands, only stopping for a bite to eat down in the rainforests. These birds used Sunday Island as a resting place on their migration to the Northern Hemisphere summer.

Our maps indicated that we had to approach the Southern Island from the west. We had learned from our charts that Sunday Island had an inlet to its beautiful coral lagoon from this direction. Once we crossed the channel, we turned "Distant Winds" towards the small pier in the middle of the lagoon. One of the beautiful things about the island was its highest mountain, Mt. Mumukai, which stood at 1,723-feet above sea level, and could be safely climbed. Its densely forested peak extended into the air, and its gently sloping sides called to us. Also significant was that since the island was so far away from the mainland, it had developed a unique eco-system. One could watch species here that were not found anywhere else in the world. We decided to go trekking the next day and climb the mountain, as we had been told of a spectacular view from the top.

We discovered that the islander's main job was to maintain a meteorological and communications station. They were mainly descended from the first prisoners who came from England and had a completely different approach to life. They acted without a rush. For some reason that was still strange to us, these people went through life at a slow pace, enjoying the simple things of their simple lives. Although it felt as if they could do more to get a higher standard of living, we knew in our hearts that they had found something that we were longing to re-discover for ourselves.

That night we went to bed early, as we would spend the next day climbing the north side of the Sunday island peak. In this paradise, the night fell like a warm breeze that gently rocked the boat from side to bottom. The ripples of the tide flowed beneath its hull. Millions of twinkling lights covered the heavens, and a full moon-shaped the silhouette of the majestic mountain we would climb the next day. Even at night, the air in the tropics was comfortable, creating an atmosphere of fascinating warmth.

Gail was staring at the horizon, slowly sipping a glass of aged red wine.

"What are you thinking?" I asked.

Without turning towards me, she replied:

"Michael, remember the first day we set sail from Auckland? For the first time in our lives, we lost sight of the shore, being alone. Remember how we had second thoughts, and we were thinking about turning back?"

"Sure, I remember," I said. "Why do you ask?"

"Can you imagine what would have happened if we had decided to go back? We would have missed all these things that we are now starting to discover for ourselves. I wonder how many people realize how important some of the decisions we make are, and how they can affect our whole lives."

"In what sense?" I asked.

"You see, before coming here, I was so busy in my own world that I never realized how far or close I was from my dreams. In my safe, daily routine, I had convinced myself there wasn't a different or better way to live my life. Yet I was so close because I always knew in my heart that a place like this existed. It was just me who was missing the whole experience by not taking the chance."

I stared at Gail. "Well, I guess we have made a decision that will probably change our lives forever, and I think we have taken a brave decision. It is easy to say that we chose well, now that everything is working well, and it is much easier to accept that what we are doing with our lives is what was meant for us. In our hearts, we now know this. But that doesn't mean that it takes courage to leave everything behind as we did, not knowing what the future will bring."

"I wonder about that, Michael. I feel that we are just making a decision we should have made long ago. I now know that the longer we wait to take a decision of this kind, the harder it gets. Without noticing it, we build a wall around us, trying to defend ourselves from the pain that can come from the outside. We don´t realize that, as we build this wall, we inadvertently leave out of our lives all these wonderful experiences. We deny ourselves the joy that dwells in all these different worlds that surround us. Maybe it's just our attitude that counts."

The gentle breeze blew stronger, and on this night of bright stars, we knew that the wisdom of Gail's thoughts would take us back to Mr. Blake's gift. The book opened, and we stared as the letters began to appear:

The choices we make

dictate the life we live.

Gail

We stared at each other in silence. Gail spoke first.

"I hope we've made the right choice, love," she said.

"I hope so too," I answered.

***

We awoke with the first rays of the sun. The skies were clear, blue as the bluest sky one can imagine. There was a long journey ahead of us, so we felt it was best to start climbing well before getting caught by the heat of the mid-day sun. We took plenty of water and some snacks for lunch and dinner. The climb would take three hours, so we thought it would be perfect to stay for lunch on the top of the mountain to restore our energies and relax with the breathtaking view.

A quarter of the way up, we left the trail and entered an opening, which led to a large cave. Sunlight appeared from the back of the cave, so it was more like a natural tunnel. A small hole in the ceiling was its source of light. I had come in through a thin opening, so I crawled and reached the other side of the tunnel, and was filled with awe at the green, unblemished portrait of nature.

I caught a glimpse of fruit.

"Gail, honey, let's go take some fruit from over there."

"Are you sure, love? What about the trail?"

"It's not that far, we'll find it again."

We walked the small distance to the fruit. They hung before me, bananas larger than any I had ever seen, yellow as the morning sun.

I took out my pocketknife and cut down a banana. I peeled it and took a bite. Its juice filled my mouth with a taste of heaven. Sweetness mixed with a refreshing; slightly sour taste made me hunger for more.

"Gail, here, try these bananas, they're great!" I said as I peeled one for her. The look of delight on her face reminded me how much I loved her. We took a few more bananas and returned to our path.

Throughout the trail, we found native species of plants that made these islands so lush, green, and unique. We saw the native yellow-flowered hibiscus, the "all-purpose plant." Its flowers are used for medicine, the leaves to cover the earth oven, the fiber for skirts, reef sandals, and ropes, and the branches for walling native cottages. The lush vegetation of the high islands included creepers, ferns, tall trees of the interior, and white coconuts, bananas, and grapefruit. Avocados and papayas were so abundant that the locals fed them to the pigs.

While we were climbing the steep mountain, the air got thinner and crisper. We saw the flamboyant trees that bloomed red during summer. Once in a while, a small bat would swirl around us, sending us to the floor, looking for cover. With the magnificent view, the animals, and the birds, we understood why it had been a long time since we had felt so close to nature, so free.

We finally reached the top of the mountain, tired, but feeling alive. Gail passed me the water bottle, and after taking several sips, we sat down, still unable to absorb the beauty of the moment.

I guess we sat in silence for what felt like an hour. I spoke first.

"Gail?"

"Yes, love?"

"Are you happy?"

She didn't turn towards me. She kept staring at the beautiful sky, with the sun already facing west, a half-moon rising in the east.

"Of course, I feel happy, being here with you, admiring so much beauty," she said. "But you know something else, Michael? I feel more than that. I feel alive once again. I think I feel the same way I did when I was a little girl." She now stared at me. "You know, believing."

I looked at her. She looked beautiful, with soft tan and deep green eyes staring at the mountains. Some of the local mynahs, a yellow-feathered bird, only found in the islands, were circling around a papaya tree.

A soft and refreshing breeze came from the west, bringing some clouds with it. We stared at each other, smiling, and without saying a word, we found ourselves back in the past, remembering...

Camping and exploring had once been our passion, playing my flute as an act of gratitude to the beauty that surrounded us. I had always known that isolation in nature, far from people and things man-made, was good for the soul. And I had learned that nature has a beautiful gift: it always gives more than what it takes.

***

With great regret, we left the peak, and started to descend the mountain.

On our way up, we had discovered a small creek that fed a beautiful blue-emerald lagoon. It was so little that it reminded me more of the water holes I had once seen in Australia, called billabongs. As night was falling, we decided to camp there. After lighting a small fire, we ate the last sandwiches we had prepared before our climb. Finally, we disposed of warm and hearty pumpkin soup, heated by the fire we had lit.

Then, something different happened. Instead of beginning a conversation, we said nothing: we just stared at each other, letting the language of love do the rest. We zipped up our sleeping bag and began getting closer and closer to each other, cuddling, and passionately kissing. It would be the first time I had made love to her with such passion for a long time. And for a brief moment, just as our bodies were about to melt like one, I felt like I was fifteen again. And I knew that Gail was thrilled once again, giving me back her love unconditionally as she hadn't done it for such a long time.

I felt the way I hadn't in years, and again remembered one of the great truths of life.

I understood that dreams were made to come

true.

***

We both smiled dreamily at each other when we woke up at sunrise. I opened the sleeping bag and walked down a couple of feet to the creek to take a bath.

"Gail, do you want to bathe in the lagoon with me?" I asked her.

"Of course!"

We stripped our clothes and showered together under the small waterfall. We played like children as the cold water splashed on our naked bodies and laughed like we hadn't laughed in a long time. As I looked at Gail, I felt brilliantly happy. After so many years, we were once again a real couple. I looked at her, unable to believe my luck at having her as my true wife.

After we finished, we gently toweled each other. We put on some clothes, lay down, and gazed at the scenery. The morning sun gently illuminated the light blue sky, free of all clouds. Lovely red and blue flowers alternated with gum trees, with leaves hanging over the green grass. Below the mountain, off in the distance, a collection of bright white huts could be seen. On the other side of the hill was clear, the calm ocean as far as the eye could see.

I turned over and gently took the book from my backpack and placed it on the lush green grass. It suddenly opened, onto a new page:

Sounds of the wind

sounds of the sea

makes one happy

just to be.

Thomas Blake

Far below lay the town where we began our journey, just yesterday, and yet it seemed an eternity away. We would now re-start our descent. I turned towards Gail as I packed my gear.

"Do you think we are rediscovering ourselves, the real Michael and Gail?" I asked.

"We are," Gail said. "Indeed we are, my love."

IX

The next day I woke up at daybreak.

We hadn't been able to sleep well that night, as "Distant Winds" jumped over choppy seas and strained against billowing winds. Long hours were spent fighting to keep "Distant Winds" on course. After descending Mount Mumukai and saying farewell to the small colony that inhabited the island, we left the Kermadec Islands. From the moment we left the reef, we encountered a powerful current flowing swiftly against us. This made navigation difficult. We both had to keep the motor at the highest setting possible to avoid it shutting down. To make matters even more complicated, a moderate swell was pushing our ship to the side. We were forced to sail in a diagonal direction to combat both the current and the swell. Near the end of the night, we began taking shifts, seeing that we wouldn't be able to sleep any other way.

Finally, the swell diminished the same way it arrived, and so did the current. Nature had tested our endurance, and I guess she was now satisfied with the way we had acted. "She decided it was time to give us a break," I thought. Now I just had to check how much we had deviated from our intended course towards Tonga.

I mixed ground coffee beans with steaming water. The refreshing smell made it almost unnecessary to drink any strong black coffee to prepare me for my turn at the wheel. Sunlight gleamed off the water, and there was a fresh, crisp smell of the ocean in the air.

I went up to the deck to check the ropes and make sure that the rudder was well placed. I saw some seagulls flying. "That's weird," I thought. We were at least 150 nautical miles from the closest land, and you usually would only see seagulls close to shore. I brought my binoculars and started searching the horizon; I didn't have to do it for very long.

Right below the sun, towards the east, there was what at first sight appeared to be a small cloud hung over the ocean. Only by straining through this white blanket could I see the island beneath it.

I went down to the cabin to check the nautical maps. I picked up my instruments to re-check my position. I repeated all the calculations just to be sure I had not made a mistake. Indeed, there was no mistake. Tonga, our next destination, was still at least five sailing days away. The island I was now staring at was not supposed to be there. However, the thought of going to land and refreshing ourselves seemed like a good idea. I gently turned the rudder and steered "Distant Winds" towards the island.

It took us almost an hour to get close to it. As I knew nothing about the island, I had to be very careful crossing the outer reef. Luckily, the swell that had rocked us during the night had vanished, which made things much more manageable. I held the wheel firmly and checked the depth of the water as I crossed the reef. In no time at all, "Distant Winds" was in the inner lagoon.

I looked for a safe place to anchor the boat. There was a lovely cozy beach of black sand in front of us, which meant that the island was of volcanic origin. I headed that way and then dropped the anchor. "Distant Winds" came to a stop.

I heard Gail's voice. She had woken up when she felt the boat stopping after the anchor was lowered.

"Is there anything wrong, love?"

"No, nothing," I said. "But now that you're awake, I think it would be a good idea for you to come up here and take a look."

She came to the upper deck. "Where are we?" she asked.

"I really don't know," I replied. "I have checked

all our maps, and this place doesn't appear in any of them. Maybe because it's too small."

We were still talking when suddenly we saw some islanders appear on the beach. There were several men, women, and children who had probably seen us sailing into the lagoon.

Behind them was a long stretch of grass that nearly reached the horizon, broken only by a thick forest. Streams and brooks of freshwater trickled over stones and mounds, gathering at the lagoon. The clouds had dispersed, leaving a bright, yellow sun and clear, blue sky. The dark-skinned islanders trekked over the sandy beach.

"What should we do?" Gail asked.

"Let's wait," I said.

The islanders approached "Distant Winds" slowly, climbing large boulders and carefully walking down the steep sand. The first to reach us was a young man of about twenty. His brown eyes spoke of happiness, and his gentle smile perfected the picture. Gleaming white teeth from an animal hung on a string around his neck, above a bare-chested body, covered only by a loincloth. He glanced quickly at the flag that hung from our mast, and then, looking back at us, asked in perfect English: "Are you Australians?"

"No, New Zealanders," Gail replied.

He said something to the other men in their own language. The rest of the group smiled, then waved good-bye and started walking back to the forest.

The man who spoke in English said: "We are very honored to be visited by New Zealanders. We don't get too many visitors around here. Are you planning to spend the night in the lagoon?" the man asked.

"Well, yes," I replied. "As long as it is not a problem for you..."

"Not at all," he answered. "In fact, we are having a traditional ceremony in our village tonight. Would you like to join us? I am sure our chief will be pleased if you could attend."

We stared at each other. "We'd love it."

"Good," he said. "Now, I will leave you to freshen up and come back for you in an hour."

"No problem," I said. "By the way, what is your name?" Gail asked him.

"Timu," he answered. "And what about you?"

"I am Gail, and this is Michael, my husband. What is the name of this island?" Gail asked.

"Numa-Numa," he said.

"We couldn't find it in our charts."

"That's true," said Timu." Nobody knows about this island, and that's the way we want to keep it. Now, I must go. I will come back to you in an hour."

***

As he promised, Timu came back an hour later. We had already freshened up and put on some clean clothes. Gail was wearing a pair of sneakers, a new white short and a blue shirt. I put on a brown t-shirt and white shorts. Being lightly dressed was perfect for the tropics' warm nights, and we were ready to cross the temperate, humid rainforest.

We started to walk through the jungle, following Timu. We had probably been walking for half an hour when we reached the village. It was designed in a circular shape, with the center used as a gathering place. All houses were made from palms and wood of the coconut tree, and it looked fresh and comfortable.

A big dinner was being prepared. Everyone helped, even the small kids, peeling the cassavas and the coconuts like experts.

Gail approached Timu.

"Timu?"

"Yes, Gail?"

"Where did you learn to speak English so well?"

"Long story," he said, "but I will try to make it short. Please sit down," he said. He then sat against a coconut tree. "When I was young, I dreamed of visiting far-away places and meeting different people. As I told you before, nobody knows about this island, and the only chance for me to experience the outer world was to leave. So one day, I got into my canoe and let the currents take me away. Several days passed until a fishing vessel heading towards what I now know was the east coast of Australia spotted me in the water and pulled me on board. When we finally arrived in Australia, I was taken to see some people in uniform. I now know they were from the Immigration Department. Still, back then, I was very scared as I couldn't understand what they wanted to know or needed from me. They were getting frustrated because they couldn't understand me. I thought about keeping it simple and repeating my name, Timu, and the name of my island, Numa-

Numa. But even then, we couldn't communicate. One of the officers brought a map thinking I could pinpoint the location of my island. Still, I had never seen a map before, and couldn't understand what they wanted me to do. In the end, they let me stay in a confinement camp while trying to find out what to do with me. I then realized that if I really wanted to learn about other people, I needed to communicate with them. From that moment, I put all my energies into learning your language. After some time, I communicated in English and explained to the officers what had happened. We became friends, and soon I was able to learn a lot about their culture. I was then allowed to apply for a visa to stay temporarily. I got a job and learned to speak fluently. I then started to save some money, so I basically got into the culture."

"So why didn't you stay there?"

"Because I never got to understand your world. You have created some wonderful technology to make life easier and safer for all, and that should give you more time to enjoy the real treasures of life. But instead, you keep being busy, always walking fast, getting in and out of trains and buses just to catch the next one, and the next one. As if enjoying life and not doing something that earned you money was a waste of time. Why do you build buildings so tall that the rays of the sun barely filter through them? Why do you call taking a break eating junk food or smoking? Why?"

"Well," said Michael, "that's a tough one, Timu, but I will try to explain why. You see, to have the things we need…"

"Need for what?" asked Timu.

"To have a better standard of living."

"Compared to what?" asked Timu. "You mean, like buying a bigger house, or a better car, things that apparently will make you feel that you have done well in life? Are these the real treasures that give meaning to your life?"

Gail stared at me, and I knew what she was thinking. Suddenly I had reacted the same way that I had done for a long time, saying things I didn't believe in. I tried to explain to this man Timu how to live a life that I knew had taken my dreams away and almost destroyed my marriage. I felt pretty ashamed of myself and Gail.

He stared towards his village. "Look at them," he said. "They are my most cherished treasures. We live a simple life, but it is real and intense. Instead of fighting each other, trying to compete all the time, we get together every time a problem arises. The children of our neighbors are treated like our own children." He stopped a child running in front of us towards a group of kids and said something in his native language to the small fellow, who answered briefly. Then Timu said something else, and the child started to laugh with the most beautiful and sincere smile. If I ever have children, I thought, I hope they will one day smile the same way.

"What did you say to him?" Gail asked.

Timu left the child on the ground, and he immediately ran towards his friends.

"I told him that you were good friends who came from far away across the ocean just to come and visit. Just to see him play". A man from the village approached Timu. After a brief talk, he turned towards us. "Everything is ready, he said, and the chief is expecting you. Please come with me."

We walked towards the center of the village. Everyone was already gathered there. The men and women surrounded an old man, seated in the middle. "He must be the chief," I thought.

Timu asked us to sit in front of the old man, and to remain by his side. They spoke about something, and when they finished talking, Timu turned towards us.

"Our chief Tamuni is very happy to have you as

guests," he said, "so we have gathered here together with you. Chief Tamuni would like to know a little more about the world you come from. I have told him about my experiences, and this has greatly increased his wisdom. Now he would like to know why you are here, so far away from your world."

Gail stared at me. "You answer," she said.

I sat comfortably over the coconut leaves they had placed for us and thought of my answer. "Well, Chief Tamuni, although your question is hard to answer, I will try to do it as simple as possible. We decided to travel around the Southern Ocean because we were getting tired of the life we were living in the city. We felt that life was passing us by, and that we were not living it the way we wanted to live it, to the fullest. We believed we had to make a decision that would make us feel alive again and give a purpose and meaning to our lives. So we started this journey some time ago, and without realizing it, we ended up here."

Timu translated these words to the chief and his people. A murmur spread among the villagers. Finally, the chief held his hand up, and everyone kept silent. He then spoke to us, but we couldn't understand. When he finished Timu translated his words:

"Chief Tamuni says that it is no coincidence what brought you here, for he had something to share with you. He says that for some people, time is the enemy that stalks their lives until they die. That's the fear that is felt by those who know they are wasting their lives. For them, time will always be their worst enemy. But for those who have finally found peace within themselves, and understood the essence of physical mortality, time becomes a silent companion. A treasure, a reminder to cherish every moment we live without taking it for granted. Indeed, time is not our worst enemy, but our best ally."

"That's easy for you to say," I replied. "You live in this wonderful paradise with no worries but to play with your children and gather the food you need. Where we come from, there is competition, greed, as one strives to be the best. We work hard to make a living and build a financial position to provide for yourself and our families in the future."

Timu referred this to the chief. He listened very seriously and then spoke to Timu. When he finished, he looked at us, smiling, waiting for Timu to translate.

"The wonderful paradise you are talking about," said Timu, "is not what you see around us, or what you see around the world you come from. It is within ourselves. Once you reach it, you won't worry about what surrounds you, because you won't have to compare or prove yourself to others. Then you will be able to choose with a true heart who you are and what you truly want to be. You will be able to build your own and unique paradise."

When Timu finished talking, the Chief Tamuni stared at us, and then said something we didn't understand.

"What did he say?" Gail asked.

"He said you will find the answer to these questions when you go back to your boat tonight and the book."

"How did he know about the book?" I asked.

Timu smiled, then said: "Our chief speaks with his heart, and he can read in your eyes the same questions he once had, questions we all ask ourselves, the ones he now knows are already answered in the book," he said. "The lonely white man who arrived at these shores many years ago, in a boat just like yours." Timu smiled and stood up. "Anyway, it is time to enjoy the feast and celebrate."

***

After a night of feasting and dancing, exotic dishes based on the local fish and vegetables abounded in and around the island. Drinking coconut milk that also gave a unique taste to all these incredible dishes. A sky of sparkling stars surrounded everywhere by the villagers. Sincere smiles, we said good-bye to the village, as Timu escorted us back to the beach where "Distant Winds" was patiently waiting for us. After reaching the shore, Timu gave us a last handshake. "It's been a pleasure having you here," he said. "Please do not tell anyone about this island. Do this, and you will always be welcomed back."

"We won't say anything to anyone," Gail said. "This, we can promise you."

"Good!" said Timu. "Bye, for now, my friends. You can stay as long as you wish in the inner lagoon."

"Thanks, Timu," I replied. As he started to disappear in the rainforest, he turned around and said:

"Don't forget to look at the book..."

Before we were able to reply, he was gone.

***

That night we stayed in the inner lagoon of this beautiful jewel of a place we had found in the middle of the ocean.

Gail prepared some tea, as we had been fed like kings during our stay in the village, playing with the children, exchanging small gifts with the elders.

"Indeed, we have been blessed with the life we are living, love," said Gail. "I would have never imagined all the new things I would experience on this journey."

"Neither did I," I replied. "Wise people can indeed be found everywhere," I said.

"Where are we heading, Michael? "Gail asked.

"What do you mean?"

"I mean, where is this adventure taking us? Remember what the chief Tamuni said about the real paradise within ourselves? I guess he was trying to teach us about the things that really matter. But what exactly was he trying to say?"

The gentle breeze came once again and softly opened our most treasured belonging. Placed in that particular spot in the upper deck. Protected from the rain, but not from the wind:

The sickness of the body can be cured for a while,

but the illness of the spirit can indeed

be incurable, as it transcends further away

than the body's death.

The sickness of the body dies with the body,

but the illness that afflicts the spirit

only dies with eternity.

Cure the sickness that afflicts your spirit,

and you will truly live forever.

Tamuni

We hugged each other, feeling that the answer to our thoughts had been given. And on that night of full moon, we kissed each other and swam naked in the lagoon's calm waters. We made love like teenagers, with the naiveté of those who see not only their eyes but also their hearts. The only witnesses to that night of true love and pure light were the dolphins, the cormorants, and the seagulls that inhabited the inner reef.

X

Traveling from one island to the next was an adventure of itself.

We spent days on end, sailing across the ocean with no human contact but ourselves. The beautiful thing about this was to be so close to nature, with Gail, as we would share our days with all the creatures that inhabited the Southern seas' skies and oceans.

We often admired the flying of the huge albatross, crisscrossing the skies, searching for that delicious mackerel that lived in this part of the world. Seagulls would follow behind, trying to get any scraps that the albatross would throw away. Once in a while, we would spot a cormorant diving into the water like an expert, never missing a fish and catching it like a professional fisherman. However, the most beautiful experience would come from the dolphins that followed us.

Dolphins of all kinds would ride the bow of the boat, jumping out of the water and then turning their bodies with their white bellies up. We learned to recognize the bottlenose, the common, the porpoise, the spotted, and many others. They would come in pods of up to a hundred, playing with the ripples that "Distant Winds" made while cruising the seas. It created a beautiful spectacle that we had never been able to watch from shore.

One day we became intrigued by a particular sound that seemed to come from the ocean's depths. In the beginning, we were not able to figure out what it was or what made it, but as the days went on, and we moved further north, we started to hear it more frequently. Then one bright morning, we saw them for the first time. They were humpback whales, creatures common to these waters that had almost been wiped out by whalers, decades ago. Now, protected by international laws, they were making a slow but steady comeback. Migrating as they had done thousands of years north from the Antarctic seas in search of warmer waters to feed and give birth to their calves.

Gail stared at the awesome giants, breaching, playing in the waves.

"Have you realized love, that basically the whales migrate all year round from one place to the other, depending on the seasons? We only see them during the fall because that's when they visit the coasts where we live in Auckland. But they really travel all year-round."

"I guess you're right," I replied. "We think that

the whales are only migrating when we see them coming to the coast of Auckland because that's where our own world is. Now we realize that there are really thousands of parallel worlds in simultaneous, and they are all real. We just see some of them, depending on where we are or what we do. We are experiencing a parallel world where we can see the humpbacks migrating north a month later than what we would normally expect back home."

Gail stared at me.

"So you think that the way we see the world depends not only on who we are but also where we are?"

"Exactly," I said. "Still, I would say that it not only depends on who we are and where we are but also to an extent on how many places we have been to. Traveling gives you a first-hand experience of what is real. I am discovering that meeting different people and discovering new places makes me see the world as it really is. It gives me different choices on how to live my own life. Once you throw away the fixed location and travel to all these places, you begin to understand the different worlds surrounding us. It really broadens your horizons."

"Gail smiled. "You mean our horizons too, Michael?"

I came close to her and kissed her. "Most of all that, Gail. I thought I had lost you forever, but now I'll do everything I can to hold you close to me forever".

She tenderly put her head on my shoulder. "Oh, Michael, I had been missing you so much and for so long," she said. "I didn't know how to find your love, but now finally I can feel you're back; the true love of my life, the man I fell in love with the first time I saw him. Don't go away again, ever. Will you promise that?"

"I won't let you alone again, Gail, ever," I said.

I looked at the majestic whale playing with her newborn calf.

"Gail, one of the things I've learned throughout this trip is that happiness doesn't exist. It's happy moments that do exist. And I suppose we really appreciate the happy moments that we experience. In that case, all those moments of true light will fulfill our lives, making it worth loving. And since leaving Auckland, I guess we have had a lot of those happy moments together, don't you think?"

In that instant, the book opened. Gail stared at me.

"Blank page," she said. "Any ideas?"

"Yes," I said, and smiled." Look again."

She looked into the open page.

> *Life is not about having things.*
> *Life is about doing things.*
>
> *Michael*

"How did you do that?" she asked. "I didn't hear you say anything."

I looked at the whales, throwing vast sprays of water through their blowholes as if agreeing with me.

"I know," I replied." I guess we are learning lots of things that can be experienced only if we follow the voice of our heart."

XI

We kept sailing for the next twelve days. Not surprisingly, with no land to block the view, we could see every sunrise and every sunset during our journey through the open seas. Just as we realized that no two islands looked the same, we saw the same was real for all the sunrises and sunsets we were now witnessing.

The heavens above us experienced incredible changes, showing us a wide variety of colors. It seemed as though a rainbow was suspended over us, and every day it was different. Sometimes, there were sharp contrasts between the fiery colors of the clouds or a subtle shift in shades of blue across the sky. After experiencing the ever-frequent violent storms of nature, rainbows would appear, sometimes two or three in a row. In no other place in the world would we have been able to experience life at its fullest most beautiful, and, most notably, at its wildest.

***

On the thirteenth day since leaving the island of Numa-Numa we finally arrived at the Kingdom of Tonga. We had plans to stop for a couple of weeks and sail around these islands.

The Kingdom of Tonga is divided into four main island groups: the Tongatapu Group in the south, with the capital Nukualofa, The Ha'pai Group, a far-flung archipelago of low coral islands with soaring volcanoes in the center, the Vavad Group, with its large landlocked harbor; and in the North, the isolated, volcanic Niuas. As our food and fuel reserves were running low, we decided to dock first at Vuna Wharf, the main port of entry to the Kingdom of Tonga and its capital. Once we had replenished our supplies and had "Distant Winds" checked for any mechanical faults or damages, we would head to the isolated Niuas. We had decided to have more time for ourselves.

We anchored at Nukualofa, Tonga's capital and busiest port, where some locals greeted us. When you see a Tongan for the first time, you understand why Tonga is called the gentle giants' land. Although they are physically big and strong, they smile like children. They have a kindred spirit and welcome all foreigners. Most of all, Tonga is its culture and people. The Tongans are exceptionally warm, relaxed, and impassive towards delays. They have a lot of fun and tease each other and sympathetic visitors always. It is said that if a Tongan loses his smile, he will slowly become cold and die.

At the end of the pier was the odd general store that carried things for people traveling like us. Usually, these stores were well supplied with local produce, which gave our trip another highlight. We were becoming experts in cooking healthy exotic dishes with products native to these tropical lands.

I left Gail with "Distant Winds" and went to the store to replenish our food supplies, and equip ourselves for the coming two weeks. This time I bought taro, yams, cassava, breadfruit, sweet potato, fish, and cooked taro leaves. I also picked up the odd wrench to replace the one about to break and other supplies such as coolant, grease, oil, and so on. After finishing my shopping, I returned to find Gail chatting with a tall Tongan man filling the boat with petrol.

I went aboard.

"Gail, I think I found everything we need."

"That's great love," she said. "Could you come here, please?"

"Sure, I replied." I jumped out of the cockpit and joined Gail and the Tongan man.

"Michael, let me introduce you to George."

"Nice to meet you, George." This man was nearly six-foot-tall and had a solid grip. I understood why Captain Cook while exploring Tonga in the famous Endeavor, told the story of how one night, a group of Tongans had given Cook's crew a lesson in boxing they never forgot.

"Good morning Michael," George replied.

"George has been working here for a long time," Gail said, "and he has met many people coming and going in sailing boats."

I immediately recognized the hidden smile in Gail's face.

"Okay, Gail, what is it?"

George turned to me. "Your wife told me that you bought this boat, Michael. Is it true?"

"Well, yes."

"Where?" asked George?

"In Auckland."

"Hmm, that's strange," George wondered. "What would 'Distant Winds' be doing in Auckland?"

"Why would that be strange?" I asked.

Gail turned to me. "Michael, I never told George the name of our boat."

"What?"

"I never told him it was called 'Distant Winds,'" Gail replied. "He basically told me that it had been a long time since he had seen 'Distant Winds' in Tonga."

"Do you remember who the owner was?" I asked George.

"Oh, it has had plenty of owners, all very nice people. I will never forget them. Never."

"Why?" I asked.

"Something in their eyes," George said." They shined differently".

"Gail and I looked at each other." Do you remember who was the first owner of 'Distant Winds'?" I asked George.

"Oh, yes," he said. "I will never forget that one. Short, good sailor but wearing the thickest eyeglasses I have ever seen."

I felt sweat on my forefront. "Do you remember his name?" I asked.

"Oh, yes, "George answered. "Mr. Thomas."

"Gail smiled at me, then started laughing. "We are definitely following the right path," she said. "Now, let's follow our own plan and go to Niuas, and discover our own trail, love. Let's try to learn to be unique, Michael. You and I."

***

It took us almost a week of smooth sailing to arrive at Niuafo'ou, the northernmost of the Niuas group of islands. If solitude was what we were looking for, then we had found it. Niuafo'ou remains one of the most isolated islands in the world. The supply ship calls about once a month, but there's no wharf on the island. For many years Niauafo'ou received its mail-in kerosene tins wrapped in oilcloth thrown overboard from a passing freighter to waiting swimmers.

This would be the perfect place to prove to ourselves how isolated we wanted to be from the rest of the world. Just the two of us, "Distant Winds," carrying our only and few earthly possessions.

***

There are not too many places left in the world where a real feeling of wilderness and isolation can be found. Niuafo'ou was undoubtedly one of these gems. Sulfuric steams, and lava trickled over a collapsed volcanic crater once 1,300-feet high. Another hole had created a barrier, which held in water, forming a lake, which, in turn, held another lake. Baths in these sulfur lagoons were the leading luxury that could be found on Niuafo'ou. The enriched volcanic soil spurred some of the largest and most colorful plants in the world.

We spent days exploring the island and its treasures. In contrast, we spent the nights aboard "Distant Winds," with the sound of the coconut trees hugging each other, just the way we did, helped by the warm breeze that came from the North.

I felt we were about to start one of those conversations I was now enjoying so much with my partner. That somehow was beginning to bring us closer than we had ever been. Now that we had rediscovered each other and recaptured our true love,

"Distant Winds" somehow served to gauge the depth of our relation to places we had never reached before. I had come to understand that this beautiful woman called Gail was a mix of many wonderful women. Some of them were just starting to blossom in the solitude of my thoughts.

"Do you believe in life after death, Michael?" she asked me suddenly.

"What?"

"I mean, do you truly think that when we leave our bodies, we will reunite somewhere else, in another place?"

"Hard to tell," I answered. "From all the experiences I have had in this past few months, Gail, I can assure you just one thing."

"And what is that?"

I stared at the full moon, right above us. "I truly believe in life before death, Gail. Not only because of what I have been able to see. But also thanks to what our friends from the book have been teaching us. Sometimes I think that they would like to come back to the world, just for an instant, just to remember why they wrote so many beautiful things about living on this planet."

I paused and then continued. "Do I think there is life after death? I don't know Gail, but I hope there is. This trip has answered questions that I thought I would never be able to answer in a lifetime. Maybe what we are not able to answer now, we will be able to answer sometime in the future. We may not know it now, but the answer is already there, waiting to be discovered."

"One thing's for sure, Gail," I continued. "I couldn't imagine my life without you. If for any reason, one of us departs before the other, then my reason to keep on living will be the thought that I will meet you once again. Somewhere, in a place where I hope we can be together for eternity."

Gail came to me and gently hugged me. I didn't say anything, but I knew she was crying. "I think we have begun to build our own Heaven on Earth, love, don't you think?"

She kissed me, then said: "No matter in what world you live, or in what time you exist, Michael Thompson, I will find you; and we will find eternity, together, you and I."

***

After three weeks of living our dreams, we were finally ready, physically, and spiritually, to leave Tonga. Even our old faithful book had helped, opening without us also looking for help,

Imagine it,

and you will achieve it.

Dream it,

and you will become it.

Trust yourself,

for you know more

than you

think you know.

Thomas Blake

The stories we'd heard, the lessons we had learned. Through the conversations we had had, the people we met up to now had replenished our sense of true self. We now knew that each new day we were living led us closer to the lifestyle and the kind of people we had always wished to be.

XII

The South Pacific is good for sailing.

There is little traffic. and no piracy, unlike the Mediterranean or Indonesian waters. The wind is a lucky charm. The standard sailing route across the South Pacific uses the Northeast and Southeast trades from New Zealand. You sail on the westerlies to a point south of the Australs, then north on the trade-winds up to Tahiti.

We would average eighty miles a day, giving us plenty of time to stay on some of the islands we liked the most, meeting the locals, and having time to learn about their culture.

Other wonders of this trip were the amount and enormity of coral reefs we found throughout our journey. Reefs of large islands, as beautiful as they are, could never match the enchantment of the smaller ones, called atolls. Covering only a minuscule portion of the South Pacific, these circular or horseshoe coral reefs bear a glittering necklace of slender inlets with luxuriant vegetation. Its waters are brimming with life. This was sprawled over their debris, which consisted of wreckage from the fierce storms of the sea. Passages through these four to six foot high atolls were usually only possible through the leeward side.

It was a bright morning when we first saw on the horizon the most southeasterly island of the 322 two islands that comprised the Fiji Islands. As we approached land, we saw a beautiful inner lagoon surrounded by an outer reef. We decided to try to find safe passage into the lagoon. I carefully maneuvered "Distant Winds" through the shallow coral that could be seen all around us. The water had turned from a deep emerald green into a completely transparent pale blue.

We finally got to the eastern part of the lagoon, where we safely anchored. I turned towards Gail.

"What do you want to do?" I asked her.

"I think we can go snorkeling," she said. "I don't think there will be any sharks around here, and if there are, they are probably harmless."

"Excellent idea!" I replied. "I'll bring the gear from the cabin." I hurried downstairs and picked up the masks, snorkels, and fins. I took it upstairs, where Gail was already waiting. We rapidly geared up, as there was no need for a wet suit in these warm tropical waters, just a shirt to protect ourselves from the intense heat and the sun. In no time we were in the water.

You haven't experienced one of the greatest joys of nature until you have explored a coral reef. One cannot walk through what would be an unaltered pristine forest because for it to be unaffected, there would have to be a lack of paths. However, it is possible to swim and feel like flying over untouched reefs, the most densely populated space on earth. A wide range of colors pervades the ocean floor, and bulges of living polyps increase the allure. Different species of fish swam to and fro through holes and crevices, and these movements of vivid color and great shapes left us amazed. A reef is created by the accumulation of millions of tiny calcareous skeletons left by multiple generations of small coral polyps, some no bigger than a pinhead. Though the frame is usually white, the living polyps have many different colors. Coral pinnacles provide a safe haven for angelfish, butterflyfish, groupers, soldierfish, triggerfish, and countless other species. Then you have the tiny octopuses and crabs, all glowing with bright colors that make the sea-bed look like the Garden of Eden. At the same time, one floats like in the air, marveling at all these beautiful creatures.

After three hours of exploring the reef, we finally got out of the water. Although we were tired, sore, and pretty severely sunburned, our eyes were still wide open with wonder at what we had seen.

We stayed inside the lagoon of that atoll for the

next three days, diving in the mornings and afternoons, playing with the fish that had now gotten used to us, and fed on our hands. Once in a while, a dolphin would swim into the lagoon, observing us and eventually coming to play. Sometimes we would spot harmless reef sharks as they cruised through the reef in search of fish. In the beginning, we had felt some anguish when we sighted one, but now we realized that this feeling was only a reaction to what we had been told about these creatures. Instead of worrying about their presence, we were starting to admire them in their natural habitat.

The second night in the atoll was one of the clear skies, with millions of stars and a full moon, the sound of the breaking surf splashing against the outer reef. Gail had prepared a beautiful meal: buttered fillets of sole fish garnished with fresh vegetables, slightly steamed and wild nuts, covered in finely shredded parmesan cheese, and a touch of garlic. A bowl of excellent local tropical fruit cut into small pieces and covered in honey completed this night's dream menu. I decided it was a perfect opportunity to open our last bottle of New Zealand Chardonnay, which we had kept for a special occasion.

"You have cooked an excellent dinner, Gail."

"Thanks, love," Gail answered. We took a sip of wine and gazed at the stars. How close we felt at that moment! As we sat alone on our gently rocking "Distant Winds," our hearts became filled with each other, and we felt the need to talk.

We stared at each other, and not finding the right words, to begin with, we turned towards our faithful book, holding hands. The wind from the west softly opened it:

To discover the truth

you need two persons:

One to say it,

and the other one,

to listen to it.

Kahlil Gibran

"Gail?"

"Yes, love?"

"I've been thinking lately about our trip."

"What about it?" she asked.

I looked at the glass of wine, thinking. "I feel great for having decided to take this trip, for having brought you back to me, and although I know we are changing for the better, there is this something in the back of my mind."

"What is it?" she asked. A shadow passed over her face.

"Well, you know, when we were working back home, I felt that we were really going somewhere, following the lead of others, doing the right thing. Now, after having been able to discover all these worlds, I don't know anymore."

"You don't know what?" Gail asked, intrigued.

"I don't know exactly what the purpose of this journey is. When we were working for our future, we had a way of measuring success, we knew what it meant for us. Now I'm not sure what success means."

Gail stared at the horizon, then said." I guess you can measure success in many different ways. I think what you are saying is that from the world we come from, success is measured by the size of the house you've got, what car you drive, and the clothes you wear. Suddenly we find ourselves in a parallel world where all these things don't matter anymore. We realize that these things are meaningful only in our society and nowhere else."

"So, what are you trying to tell me?"

"That we are successful, Michael. We chose to take this journey with no idea of what the future would hold for us. And now, I wouldn't change these moments we have lived for all the riches in the world. I consider myself rich enough in having you, in the person I am becoming, and in being able to witness the wonders of the world. Don't forget that there is no predetermined or marked path ahead of us, Michael. We are building our own unique path, with no guidance but one of our own instinct and the strength of our love. I think that is something."

She was right. There was nothing that could be more important than the moments we were living in. All the money in the world couldn't buy what we were feeling inside. And we had started to realize that we could feel the same way anywhere, maybe even back home, because something was changing inside of us. We could always be the persons we wanted to be, in any place. So long as we kept our eyes open to the essential things in life, we were learning to identify throughout this trip.

The gentle breeze from the west came again, as

Gail and I stared at each other, smiling. The book opened on a new page.

The key to happiness

is having dreams.

The key to success

is making those dreams

come true.

Gail and Michael

"We both did it this time," I said. "We were thinking the same, and the sum of our thoughts is reflected in this page."

"I know," Gail said. "I guess we are starting to be one, you and I." We stopped talking and kissed. We knew we had a wonderful dessert coming up.

XIII

In the open ocean, we learned many things from the wind.

Like a seagull with open wings, we watched "Distant Winds" traveling through the idyllic Fijian islands. Some so small, they could hold only a single coconut tree. "Distant Winds" would sometimes run with the wind, sometimes against it. It was then that we realized that it is not the way the wind blows but how we raise the sails that give direction not only to our destiny but also to our dreams.

We learned what we had known in theory for a long time. The actual wind, the wind that blows when nothing interferes with it, is modified by the forward motion of the boat. This wind, when the ship is moving, is called the "apparent wind." As long as the boat you are sailing on moves, the wind you are dealing with is the apparent wind. If you can understand the apparent wind and the turning moment of the sails, you can become a good sailor.

At night we learned to recognize the Southern Cross. This beautiful array of stars is taken for navigational purposes to be stationary in the sky, facing south. It is sufficiently correct to allow the movement of all other heavenly bodies to be considered relative to the Southern Cross. It's the constant celestial navigation in the Southern hemisphere.

The azimuth became our guide; this is the bearing of a heavenly body from the observer's position. The azimuth angle and the azimuth circle became part of our daily routine. We had to be taken into account every time we set course, blending our nautical charts with the sailing knowledge we were acquiring on this spiritual journey.

We learned a lot, and although we had to trust our sailing abilities to be sure of our course, we had also started to sail by instinct and not by rule. We had learned to follow the sun during the day, and the moon during the night. We observed the seagulls facing the changes in the wind as we approached land. We watched the whales and dolphins as they traveled the immensity of the ocean. They had become our guides, our navigational charts. Everything that surrounded us had suddenly become part of ourselves. The love we were sharing had become part of this flow. It was incredible for Gail and me to realize that all the things we were now experiencing had always been there, just waiting for us to discover them.

***

We had occasionally experienced sharp rain showers during our trip, but always near an island. The first time that the rain fell in the open ocean was a day of self-discovery for us. There was no storm or rough seas, just the sound of raindrops pouring from the sky, hitting the "Distant Winds'" deck by the millions. In the city, we would run for cover in order not to get wet. The rain started to fall. We went to the open deck to feel the rainfall over us, as it really was. To get wet with pure water and symbolically cleanse ourselves.

Suddenly I realized Gail had an extraordinary experience. Her eyes were wet, not with rain but tears, and she glows in the pouring rain.

"What is it?" I asked

"I can feel the presence of God. He is in the rain and the sea, and I can feel him. I can see Him."

"What does He look like? "

She stared at the horizon. "He looks like a dolphin, you know? And He also looks like a whale. He speaks like the wind, as well as the thunder. He whispers dreams to us, even though we sometimes don't listen. He is within the sunrise and the sunset.

He is in every star we watch at night. And in this magical solitude we have achieved, my love, He reminds me of all the good things in life: pure and beautiful."

She paused as her tears melted with the crystal clear rain in one single truth.

"Remember what we learned about God in school — a God of fire and punishment? I don't believe in that God anymore. Times are changing, Michael, and right now, in the truth of what my eyes can see, my heart can feel, and my soul can understand, I can see what God really is. And you know something? God has nothing to do with religions. He has to do with beauty, with the truth. Because beauty is truth, and the truth is beauty."

Gail grabbed my hands and held them tight. "You know what I have realized, love? Hell doesn't exist. It's not a place or time. Hell is not enjoying all the beautiful things that are available to us, the things that we are starting to discover. Hell is not able to appreciate the things God has given us to enjoy and cherish forever."

I was getting a little scared, hearing Gail speaking this way. There was still something inside of me that refused to believe her, to listen to her. I had been taught since I was a child that was completely different from what Gail was saying. I suddenly felt that it was almost a sin to listen to her.

The book opened, there in the middle of the rain:

You see things,

and you say

Why?

But I dream things

that were never seen,

and I say,

Why not?

Gail

"What is happening to you, Gail?" I asked, afraid.

"Something wonderful," she replied. "Believe me, love, this is the first time I have really seen the rain falling. It is the first time I have heard the voice within me, telling me who I really am." She came to me and gave me a soft kiss.

"I love you, Michael," she said, "as much as I love to be alive." She looked at me with those beautiful green eyes and then stared at the ocean.

"I have finally opened my wings, my love," she said." I have finally learned to fly. And nothing will ever be able to close them again. Nothing."

She stared at the horizon.

"Some people live their dreams, Michael. Some people don't, and they close their eyes forever to the truth. I guess only God knows why. I just know I will never close my eyes again. Never."

XIV

Ten days after leaving the last Fijian island, we arrived at Vanuatu, a long necklace of alluring islands. Vanuatu means "land eternal," stretching from north to south hundred miles from the Torres Islands and east of New Caledonia, our next destination. The islands were lush green, covered in a green blanket. The blue sky offered a sharp contrast to the luxuriant green archipelago but melded with the ocean. Beautiful specks of white seemed to be foam at first, but upon close examination turned to be enchanting coral reefs with vividly colored fish swimming to and fro. In these areas, so close to land, the water's shallowness and the reflection of the sunlight combined to produce an entrancing emerald color. A soft breeze helped mitigate the hot and humid air that prevailed in this part of the South-Pacific.

It had been almost two weeks since we had seen signs of civilization. Although we had mixed feelings about arriving at a place where we could see all the things of modern life, it was also a blessing. We had to refuel the boat and buy groceries and other supplies that we needed to continue our journey.

I had never forgotten what my mother had once

told me long ago: "Don't forget, Michael, that important as it is to have your dreams close to the stars, so it is equally important to have your feet well placed on the ground."

"Indeed, there is nothing wrong with modern life," I thought. "To find an equilibrium between what nature can teach you and the good things that society can offer you, without getting trapped in a world where only material things count."

I went into the main store in the town. The place was well supplied with fresh tropical fruit, as well as local vegetables. At a gas station, a man looked under the hood of an old automobile. In contrast, another man, probably its owner, stood beside him. Kids wearing only shorts were running everywhere, with that fresh smile that only children have. Some young men were unloading groceries from trucks parked in front of the general store, probably the produce of their farms. I took out my list and started buying all the things that we needed for the next part of our trip, New Caledonia.

Beautiful local produce, like freshly harvested carrots, onions, sweet potatoes, and okra, made my shopping enjoyable. Bargaining was the name of the game in these lands and didn't seem to bother anyone. It was just part of the local culture.

I paid for the groceries and was about to leave the shop when I saw a public phone, the first I had seen in weeks. Now that I thought about it, I had almost forgotten that phones existed.

An idea came to me. "I'll call Mr. Blake and tell him how happy I am for deciding to make this journey and to thank him for the book he had given us as a present. That was helping turn this trip into such a wonderful adventure.'

I purchased a phonecard and read the instructions on the phone booth about making a long-distance call. I checked the time difference between Auckland and the cosmopolitan capital of Vanuatu, Port Vila. Yes, Mr. Blake's bookstore was definitely still open. I decided to call him.

For a while, the phone rang until a female voice that I didn't recognize answered at the other end.

"May I help you?"

"Yes, good morning. May I speak with Thomas Blake?"

"Excuse me?"

"May I speak with the owner of the bookstore, please?"

"May I ask who is calling?"

"Yes, this is Martin Thompson, a friend of Mr. Blake."

There was a long silence on the other side of the line. "Could you wait for a second, please?" said the lady. Then I heard the woman speaking with someone else. I couldn't recognize her voice, either. She took the phone.

"Good morning Mr. Thompson, were you asking for Mr. Blake?"

"Yes, Madame." I was starting to get annoyed. This was a long-distance call, and I was wasting time and money." Now, could you please pass the phone to him?"

There was silence for an instant, then she said: "We are sorry Sir, this is not a bookstore anymore. It is now a coffee-shop."

I was surprised by the news. "Since when? "I asked

"Well, it's been two months now since the owner of the bookstore got sick."

"Thomas?"

"Were you a close friend of him?"

"Well, not really, but we were friends. I used to

buy books from his bookstore."

Then came a long silence.

"Sir, I don't know if this is the right time to tell you."

"Tell me what?"

"The owner of the bookstore passed away a month ago," she said. "I know this because the lady that worked with him has applied for a job here. She really needs it. She is so sad about his death."

I kept silent. I didn't know what to say.

"Sir? Are you still there?"

I couldn't answer. I carefully hang the phone. I could only think about the last words Mr. Blake had said to me when leaving his wonderful bookstore for the last time.

Have a beautiful life, Michael...

I closed my eyes, still in disbelief. "He knew we wouldn't see each other again," I thought.

***

Coastal clouds slowly began to roll across the morning sky, turning silver with the sun's reflection. As the rain started to pour from the heavens, I took my wallet and groceries and started strolling back to the boat. I needed a drink, and I didn't want to be alone.

I spoke with Gail and gave her the news as gently as I could. At first, she was very sad and started crying. But then she began to calm down.

"Do you think it had to be like this?" she asked.

"What do you mean? "

"Well, can you imagine what would have happened if we had returned from our trip and seen Mr. Blake? What would he have said to us to explain the book?"

Gail had a point. How would Thomas Blake explain the magic that dwelled in the book he had given to us as a present?

"I guess you are right, love," I said. "It would have been perfect if we could go back and talk to him, now that we know he was such a special person, some kind of angel. But I guess things don't work when the timing is not right. Maybe there were things he knew that we are not supposed to know yet; maybe his mission was finished, and he had to go. And besides, if he was an angel, what is the difference between disappearing or leaving his physical body?"

Gail stared at me. "Maybe you're right. Maybe this is the way it had to be. It's just that I still don't understand so many things about life."

The gentle breeze once more filled the deck of "Distant Winds," The book opened, once again:

When does somebody really die?

When we stop thinking about him.

And when does somebody really depart?

When we stop remembering him.

Michael

"Do you think he has turned into an angel?" Gail asked.

I didn't have time to answer. The book turned to the next page, and we stared at it, with tears in our eyes.

People die not

when they are buried

in their grave,

but when they finally

give up

their dreams.

Thomas Blake

"He has turned into an angel right, love?" Gail asked.

I wiped the tears from my eyes, hugged her with all my strength, and then smiled.

"I have no doubts," I said.

XV

Vanuatu was the most northerly point we would reach on our trip.

We had seen more than 3,500 miles of ever-varying splendor and beauty since we left Auckland. From picturesque islands to resplendent coral reefs and small, intensely colored fish swimming in shallow water to a pod of whales, singing and calling to each other. We had experienced many types of weather, from the glorious sunset on a clear day to an incessant rain pattern. Still, most importantly, we had found ourselves and each other. No longer did we determine how happy we were by how many possessions we had because now we knew we had each other, and that was more than enough. And as one day, we suddenly decided to start this magical adventure without knowing what the future would hold. We suddenly felt it was now time to return to Auckland, to where we belonged.

As we turned the sails of "Distant Winds" towards the south, we saw a majestic albatross. He also seemed to have realized that he had traveled further north from its domains than it intended. We now had to head back to the southern seas, to where he also belonged.

The moment turned mellow, and in the vastness of the ocean, a feeling that resembled sadness filled our hearts. A thunderstorm was raging far on the horizon, turning the afternoon light so luminous gold. I wish I could have bottled it and kept it forever.

"Don't feel sad, Gail," I said, trying to comfort her." It's not the end of the trip. We are just turning south, but we still have plenty of adventures ahead of us."

She looked at me, then said, "I'm not sad, Michael. I'm just a bit mellow, and I am enjoying this moment. I have learned that we don't necessarily have to laugh to feel happy or cry to feel sad. I am just accepting what I feel right now, and although I'm not happy, I feel well." She smiled at me and held my hand, her green eyes shining like emeralds.

"Do you remember what Mr. Blake wrote at the beginning of the book he gave us as a present? He told us to fill our days with happiness and our nights with dreams. And once those dreams had become a reality and turned into sweet memories, that we should never forget them. That's precisely what I am experiencing right now. I remember all those beautiful moments we have shared, those moments that will never come back, that is gone forever, but will never be forgotten. Because you know what? We really live two parallel lives, Michael, the one we actually live, and the one we will always remember. And both lives are real and strong.

I tried to follow her thoughts. "So, what are you saying, Gail? That these mixed feelings of mellowness and sadness are just part of what we are supposed to feel right now, and that we should look at them as part of the changes that are happening inside us?"

She smiled. "Remember all those stories we have heard or read that involve people having near-death experiences? Whether they are true or not, people who have been close to death have a special light in their eyes. Most of them don't fear death anymore, yet they immediately rearrange their priorities in life. Suddenly things that used to be important, such as a good financial position, are no longer. Family, friends, helping others, becomes their priority. It's like realizing that all the things we take for granted are not really there forever. That is precisely what is happening to us through this journey. We are learning that there is nothing wrong with being financially successful. So long as you give it the importance, it really deserves. It should never compromise the precious time you should use to become a real human being.

"This is a tough one, Gail," I said. "Do you think

our friends can help us do this?" I asked.

"Sure," Gail replied. "Let's concentrate and see what they have to say."

We held our hands in silence, watching the sails of "Distant Winds" take us towards our destiny.

The gentle breeze came, opened the book, and then disappeared the same way it came.

We stared at the book, still holding hands. This page contained two sayings:

From all the paths you can choose in life,

there is one

more important

than all others.

It is the one that will change you

into a true human being

Thomas Blake

A man is rich

in proportion

to the number of things

he can afford

to let alone.

Thoreau

We sat in silence. Gail had been right. Now we had finally realized that this experience was turning us into pure human beings, enjoying every moment, learning day to day, knowing each other better, watching the world with true eyes, and with true light.

We also knew that these mixed feelings we felt were caused by our knowledge that sooner or later, we would have to return to the world we had come from. How would we react? Would we see things differently? Would we be accepted the way we were now? Was it really essential to be approved by others?

Would we ever be the same again?

XVI

On a clear night, the Southern Cross looks like a cluster of jewels in the Southern sky.

The pointer stars, Alpha and Beta Centauri, make it easy to identify the Southern Cross positively, as they point directly at it. To position yourself in the open sea, you follow the Cross's long axis towards its furthest star. That's is where the real south is. Follow that direction five times the longer axis of the Cross, and you'll find the South Pole.

Not a cloud was in the sky, allowing us to watch the heavens' full splendor and glory. Stars shimmered and danced in the night sky as the full moon hung majestically overhead, splashing its intense, light against the mirror that is the sea.

We headed south-west. A small deviation towards the west to find the shorter route towards our next stop, the French islands of New Caledonia, which lay 400 miles away. If we were lucky enough to keep getting the northerly winds in the next few days, we would average 80 miles per day, which would take us to New Caledonia in no more than a week.

Sailing by night was an experience in itself. Not being able to use our natural senses to see where we were heading, we had to rely on our knowledge of the stars and our navigational equipment. However, without noticing it, we had started to develop some intuition that let us know well in advance if something was not going well. Just like a blind person can sense smells and sounds that ordinary people cannot detect, we started to see things not with our eyes but with our instinct.

There was one particular occasion that clearly illustrated this transformation. We were together on the lower deck, playing cards, and listening to some soft music. An hour before, we had set the sails on a predetermined course. As the wind had been behaving splendidly, we felt assured that nothing would go wrong. We knew that we were still several hundred kilometers from New Caledonia.

Suddenly Gail put the cards down.

"Anything wrong, love?" I asked.

"Didn't you hear it?"

"Hear what?" I asked puzzled.

"That sound."

"What sound?"

"Michael, please turn the music down."

I did what she asked. "Do you hear it now?".

"No," she said. "I think it's gone."

"Never mind," I said. "Maybe you just thought it. Come on, let's go on with the game. It's probably one of your tricks, now that I'm winning."

I couldn't keep talking. I felt a sound I couldn't distinguish but knew was real. The funny thing is that it came from within me as if trying to warn me about something.

Gail saw my eyes. "You're feeling the same anxiety, aren't you?" she asked.

I stood up. "Let's go up. Something isn't right.

We went to the upper deck and started to look around us. The night was as peaceful as we had left it an hour ago. Yet, something was not right. I turned on the main light beam of "Distant Winds" and head it straight in front of us.

We couldn't believe our eyes. A hundred yards in front of us, I could count at least ten or twelve humpback whales, coming straight. I had heard stories of how these giants of the sea could snap the keel of a sailing boat with no trouble.

"Blow the horn, Gail!" I shouted desperately. "We have to let them know we're here."

Gail started blowing the horn relentlessly while I began turning on all the lights I could find. The pod was now dangerously close to us and could hit us at any instant.

"Gail, fasten your safety harness, now!" I did the same and waited for the worst.

The next few minutes lasted an eternity, as the whales passed around and below "Distant Winds." It seemed that we had acted right just at the last minute, and the pod had been able to detect us. The main male had detoured from its collision course, and the rest had followed, and now we could see with great relief that the pod had passed around "Distant Winds."

We took off our safety harnesses and made one last check to ensure there were no more whales around. We also decided to leave some lights on, just in case. Then we sat down on the upper deck. I helped myself to a bit of brandy; it really brought me back.

"Gail, what happened? Did you feel that same anguish coming from inside you?"

"Yes, Michael. At first, I thought it was some

kind of sound, but then I realized it was coming from within me, as trying to warn me about something."

Well, it definitely worked!" I said. "Whatever it was, it sure saved our lives. But what made us do what we did and react the way we reacted?"

The gentle breeze this time came from the North, opening our most cherished possession.

A cloud does not know why

it moves in such a

direction and at such a speed.

It feels an impulsion,

this is the place to go now

But the sky knows the reasons and the patterns

behind all clouds,

and you will know, too,

when you lift yourself high enough

to see beyond horizons.

Richard Bach

We stood in silence, knowing that what had to be said had been said.

After a while, Gail spoke.

"Michael,"?

"Yes, love?"

"Did I ever tell you that I was frightened when still a kid because I thought I could hear some voices or feel things that others would call strange?"

"Yeah, I know the feeling," I replied. "I guess that when you are younger, your pure heart can absorb all the messages that come from within, but with time we start losing them until we finally call them spooky experiences."

Gail smiled. "My teacher in school used to call these things, the bad strays, the weeds we should pull out of our systems if we wanted to be saved."

"Isn't it funny," I replied, "how sometimes ignorance or fear of the unknown can make you judge things terribly wrong."

Without saying anything, our precious book opened once again.

I have always been regretting

that I was not as wise today

like the day I was born.

Thoreau

Gail smiled. "Do you know what I would tell my old teacher if I saw her, right now?"

"Tell me."

"I would tell her that I had taken the journey of a lifetime. A journey that changed me by showing me the truth that lies before those who seek. Those who learn to hear from within themselves. The bad stray that had wandered into my heart, as my teacher had taught me. A weed among her kind had become the favorite flower in the fields of my heart."

XVII

A week went by. We gazed at the horizon, we could see majestic mountain peaks, high in the sky, offering a sharp contrast to the flourishing meadows and forest just below them. We set sight for these splendors of nature that formed New Caledonia.

The islands were still French territory, so we thought there would be a lot of French influence in the islanders' culture. It had been one of those places where the fusion of the local and foreign cultures had gone smoothly, and the people had lived in peace for a long time.

A gentle breeze coming from the east helped us reach the outer reef of the most significant island, Grand Terre, in an hour. It took us almost half an hour to reach the main marina of Noumea, a thriving port of the South Pacific and the capital of New Caledonia. As the island had no industry other than tourism, everything had to be brought in by plane or ship.

Gail and I had planned to spend a couple of weeks in this idyllic place, exploring the local culture and the natural beauty of the island. However, we decided first to restock our supplies of food and fuel that had been dwindling fast.

While Gail washed away the salt off "Distant Winds" with the help of a water hose from the marina, I went to the main store that was pretty close to the pier. There, people of all races were doing their daily shopping. The variety of fresh fruit was astonishing.

After buying our food supplies, I went into a hardware store, as we had to change some of the ropes that had been badly damaged by the strong winds that had hit us two days ago. My manual compass had also been damaged, so it was necessary to purchase a spare one. I asked for the ropes and compass that needed to be replaced.

"Just arrived on the island?" a man asked me.

"Well, yes," I said.

"Are you the owner of 'Distant Winds'?"

"Yes, that's me," I replied.

"Welcome to New Caledonia," he said. "My name is Alec, and I've been living on these islands for a long time. Believe me, you won't regret having stopped here."

I looked at the man. He had a dark complexion because of the intense sun that prevailed in this part of the world. He was definitely of European origin, tall, and probably French because of his accent when speaking in English. Although I had just met him, he seemed to me to be a good and honest person.

"So, you live in Noumea?" I asked.

He smiled. "Oh no, not at all. Living in Noumea is like living in the city, and if I'd wanted that, I would have stayed in Paris. No, I live in the mountains surrounding the east coast of the island, about thirty miles from here, with Sophie, my wife."

"So how come you left Paris?"

He smiled again. "You probably know the reason as well as I do."

"To live life to the fullest? To break the cycle and discover the really important things in life? To find out who you truly are?" I asked.

He cracked up laughing." I couldn't have said it better," he said. He paused and said: "Would you like to have dinner with my wife and me this evening? I hope you will excuse my wife's broken English. You can then spend the night with us, and I will bring you back to your boat first thing in the morning. We would be delighted to have some company."

"Well, I'll have to check with my wife to see if it's okay with her."

"Of course," said Alec. "I'll be staying in town all

morning, and you can leave me a message here at the hardware store with Michelle, the owner. She is an excellent friend of mine."

"Thanks, Alec, I'll do that," I said. We shook hands and said goodbye. I paid for the ropes and compass and started walking towards the door. As I was about to leave the shop, I imagined myself asking Gail about the invitation to dinner. "You know I would love it," she would say.

I stopped.

Wasn't one of the reasons for this trip to start getting to know each other better, to trust our hunches, and the way we knew each other? How could we do this if we kept thinking the way we did in our old life, always asking for permission? Doing things mechanically, instead of instinctively?

I turned back and walked towards Alec. "I'm sure my wife would love to have dinner with you and Sophie. We gladly accept your invitation."

"Trés bien!" said Alec in his perfect Parisian French. "We will pick you up from the marina at five o'clock this afternoon.

"Thank you. We look forward to spending the evening with you and your wife," I said.

***

As I had expected, Gail was delighted about having dinner with another couple with whom we knew we had things in common. Besides loving French cuisine, it would be great to be guests after having cooked meals for so long. We also thought it would be suitable for "Distant Winds" to take a well-deserved rest; to fold its wings and rest for a while.

As promised, Alec arrived at the pier at five o'clock. I introduced him to Gail, and then we got into his four-wheel drive and started heading towards the east side of the island.

Once we left Noumea, we got onto the island's main road, which ran parallel to the coast. We were treated to a breathtaking view of the island, with steep verdant mountains stopping at cliffs, which led straight down to powerful waves crashing and playing against these rock walls. Here and there, we would see a small beach far below, sometimes consisting of white sand, and others of black, revealing the mixed origins of the island.

We had traveled around thirty miles when Alec took a detour onto a dirt road that went inland towards the mountains. "This is where the trail starts going up," he said. "We will ascend nine hundred feet before reaching my home."

He wasn't exaggerating. The road began meandering as it got steeper and steeper, confirming the need for four-wheel drive vehicles on the island. Apart from the main road, all other ways were barely trails, or dirt roads flattened every so often and had to be re-built when the rains washed them away.

"We are almost there," said Alec. He finally took a sharp curve and stopped the car. "Voila!" he said.

The trail stopped in what must truly paradise look like. In the middle of a rainforest, hemmed in by imposing trees on all sides, was a pasture covered by grass as green as the purest emerald. Beams of light filtered through the tall timber to reveal exotic wildflowers, ranging from pristine blue to vivid red. In the middle of these enchanting blossoms was a small wooden house. Horses peacefully roamed and grazed in the idyllic scene.

The door of the house opened, and a thin, blond woman appeared waving to us.

"Alec, I was waiting for you," she said.

"Bon Soir, Sophie," he said. "I had to fix the car's fuel pump, so it took me a little longer." He then looked at us. "Let me introduce you to a couple of

New Zealander friends that have just arrived at the islands. I thought it would be a good idea to welcome them with a French dinner."

"Of course!" she said, in her broken English. 'When did you arrive?" she asked.

"This morning," answered Gail. "We have been traveling for quite some time since leaving Auckland and wanted to visit New Caledonia, so we finally arrived this morning in 'Distant Winds.'"

Sophie's face suddenly changed.

"You said 'Distant Winds'?"

"Yes," answered Gail." That's the name of our boat. "Is there anything wrong?"

Alec and Sophie stared at each other, then smiled. "Not at all," they said. "Now, please come in and let's have a glass of wine in the verandah."

***

We spent the next hours talking about our lives. Gail helped Sophie prepare beautiful mahi-mahi, a local fish in the French style, simmering it in sweet white wine, then spreading it with local herbs and spices. As usual, with French cuisine, the dinner was superb. We washed the white, spicy fillet á la Meniere with a delicate, chilled white Burgundy wine. Finally, Sophie brought some freshly brewed coffee produced in the islands. It tasted superb.

"So, what made you guys settle in this part of the world?" Gail asked Sophie and Alec.

"Well, said Sophie. Look around you. This is a place where you really smell the flowers. You can really taste the fruit, which grows naturally, and you can see the beauty of the sea and the mountains, and millions of stars at night. Many places are beautiful, but you need a special attitude to be able to enjoy them. We couldn't do that at home."

"When we were living in France," said Alec, "we didn't have the time to pay attention to all these things. We were too busy involved in our business, always running, always needing more time to do the things we thought were important. One day we suddenly realized that we had chosen a life based on the options that had been made available to us in the city we lived in. And we realized that there should be many more options to live the life we wanted to live."

Alec lit a cigar, and after politely declining to his offer of giving us one, continued. "In Paris, we didn't have much time to discover the world. So we took a drastic decision, and one night we decided that enough was enough; that we had to take a chance, as we felt life was passing us by. We sold everything we had, and we bought our plane tickets to New Caledonia. Once we stepped down from the airport, smelled the humid hot air, and saw the green islands for the first time, we knew we had taken the right decision."

"When was this?" I asked.

"Ten years ago," said Alec. "We found this piece of heaven on Earth, thanks to a friend of ours. We built the house ourselves, bought some horses, and started to grow some of our food. Imagine the small budget involved living under these conditions, so what would probably represent a financial problem in France is not one here."

Suddenly we heard a horse galloping outside the house. A few seconds later, a small boy, probably eight or nine years old, entered the room.

Sophie said something in French to the boy. He then slowly approached us.

"Bon Soir, Madame. Bon Soir, Monsieur," he said and smiled, then ran into the kitchen.

Gail and I stared at each other." Your son?"

"Yes," said Alec. "His name is François. He was born on the islands."

"But isn't it a problem for you?" Gail asked. "I mean, what about the school, safety..."

Sophie smiled. "Gail, in this simple world, the things that are problems in the world we came from are not. There is a small school in the village, ten minutes by horse from this place. We use the jeep only to go to town, so we learned to ride horses; it is much simpler and doesn't pollute the rain forest. They don't cost us much, as they feed on the local plants, and they are free to roam. Francois learns about his French background or anything else we consider useful from the world we came from. We teach him ourselves. He has lots of friends who live around us and go to the same school, and regarding safety, what do you think could happen? Why would someone want to harm him? In these cultures, children are precious, the most treasured thing someone can have, and all are looked after by all the adults."

Alec went to the window and gazed at a brilliant full moon. "Can you think of any better start in life than the one we give to our son? When he is older, we will take him to France, where we come from, to the world we left behind. Then it will be his decision where to live or what to do. But he will possess a treasure that most of us never had."

"What will that be?" I asked.

"He will have a choice, for he has seen the world in its true dimension, and because of this, our son will be able to trust his heart, and what he has seen with his own eyes. It's funny. There is no perfect world, Michael and Gail, but you can make your own a little better every day. We have no complaints about our beautiful New Caledonia, although sometimes we miss our traditional France. I guess it's just a matter of putting both places in a balance and then making a choice."

He paused. "Many people around the world will tell you that they know what they want from life. Yet what they don't realize is that they are only considering limited options. They have decided to become in life, not necessarily what they really want to be, as they have never seen different worlds, different options. Doesn't it ring a bell to you that most of the time, the son of a doctor will want to be a doctor? That the son of an architect will want to be an architect? I guess part of it is genetically inherited, but that doesn't mean that it has been made personally. To decide, you have to make a choice. And to choose, you have to have options. And to be free to consider the options, you have to take risks, and listen to the voice that comes from within."

Gail and I stared at each other. There was nothing else to say, as this beautiful couple living in this magical place had said everything that mattered. And most importantly of all, they lived the way they spoke.

"A votre santé!" said Alec.

"Cheers!" we replied.

We emptied our glasses. Then Sophie asked Alec: "Do you think this is the right time to ask them?"

"I cannot think of a better moment," Alec said.

"Ask us what?" said Gail.

"Alec told me that the name of your boat is 'Distant Winds.' Did you name it yourselves, or did it already have that name?"

"We named it ourselves. Well, not really ourselves, but we took the name from someone we know."

"Do you keep a book in a wooden box in your boat?"

We couldn't believe what we were hearing. "How do you know?"

"Remember we told you that a friend of ours showed us this place twenty years ago? The locals say that this man arrived at the island on a boat called 'Distant Winds.' They say one day he disappeared for two years and that nobody could find him, although 'Distant Winds' was anchored at the pier. It seemed he came up to the mountains to think in solitude. When he finally returned, the islanders thought he was crazy, as he kept opening a book full of blank pages, as if he was reading it."

"Blake," I said. "It was he."

"Yes," said Alec. "Thomas Blake showed us this piece of paradise, and he did something better still."

"What was that?"

They stared at each other, smiling. "He taught us to read the book. Where others saw only emptiness, we learned to see with our hearts."

We couldn't speak. Everything was happening too fast. There were too many coincidences. Coincidences? Not at all. I had now learned that what we call coincidences are just things that happen when we are doing what we are supposed to do.

"We are starting to learn how to read the book," Gail said.

"I know," answered Sophie. "I can see it in your eyes. I can also see in your eyes that you are beginning to write in it. And believe me, when you go back tomorrow to your beloved "Distant Winds," you will be able to read more pages."

We looked at each other in silence, thinking about the man who had done so much for us.

"Let's make a toast," Alec said." Any suggestions?"

"To our good friend Thomas Blake!" I replied.

"To the joy of life," Gail said.

Sophie and Alec gazed at each other, then said warmly:

"To the 'Distant Winds' that brought us all together."

XVIII

It had been more than six months since we had left our beautiful Auckland searching for the answers to our questions about life, about ourselves, and about our love.

Sometimes we thought it would be hard to restart the kind of life we had lived before. We couldn't go back to the lifestyle we had, now that we had discovered the way we wanted to live our lives. Although we started the trip as an adventure, it was now becoming clear that this trip was not only an adventure anymore but also a different way to face life. We had taken risks. Now, free of all the things we had once surrounded ourselves with, we had started to recognize the essential elements in our lives, the ones that can only be felt and shared but never possessed. But most of all, it had brought Gail back to me.

"Distant Winds" was now starting to change colors, as the winds of the Southern seas and the salt, dried by the burning sun, acting as a strong catalyst that corroded parts of our boat. It was time to give it the thorough clean up and the fresh coat of paint it deserved. We decided to commission someone at our next stop, take care of the sails, check the hull of the boat, and the keel.

We had recently been discussing plans to start a family, something we had not even thought about during the trip. It seemed that, now, at the end of our journey, the words that Gail had said well before we left New Zealand had acquired meaning: that soon we would definitely be better parents for our children, now that we were living the life we had always wanted to live, with memories of a trip that we would cherish forever, and now that our strong love had blossomed once again. We could show them the different choices that life gives to each of us at an early age and show them how to choose with an open mind and heart which path to take, regardless of what others might think. And who knows, maybe we could make another trip with them to show them all the parallel worlds that exist, and how each one has a lesson to teach us.

We had a whole world to show to our children when the moment was right. Like Alec and Sophie, we would be able to give them an excellent chance to learn to distinguish between a life they were supposed to live and one they truly wanted to live.

***

After sailing all morning, we finally entered the reef that surrounded the eastern side of Norfolk Island. From this point, we could see houses that looked familiar to our beloved Auckland, as Norfolk Island was an Australian dependence, inhabited by white settlers from England and Australia. Today the island is a favorite vacation spot for Australians and New Zealanders. This island was already inhabited when "discovered" by Captain Cook in 1774. First established as a British penal colony, it was then used to resettle the Pitcairn islanders, the descendants from Tahitian women, and English sailors. They had arrived at these coasts in the infamous Bounty, an English boat that committed mutiny while sailing in the Southern Ocean.

Finding things so familiar to our beloved New Zealand gave us the feeling that we were already home. A pod of playful dolphins happily greeted us with leaps and clicking sounds. We made our way into the inner reef and came closer and closer to the beautiful seashore, covered with flourishing plants and sparse palm trees. The shallow but enchanting reef, teeming with life, protected the island and "Distant Winds" from the foaming surf.

We anchored the boat late in the afternoon, close to a beautiful, crystal clear waterfall that sprung from the top of a cliff. It made rainbows appear and disappear as the water turned into a spray of tiny droplets of different colors. The view was magic and familiar. We decided to spend the rest of the day in "Distant Winds," that old boat we had purchased in Auckland long ago, and that now felt like home, one that we had learned could take us anywhere we wanted, as long as we were determined enough.

"Gail?"

"Yes, love?"

"I've been thinking."

"About what?"

I sat down on the upper deck and looked up at a million stars, a bright orange moon glowed wonderfully. "I have been thinking a lot about Mr. Blake, and what's happened to us on this trip. Although I think I understand what he was doing with his life, I still can't fully understand the reason why it had to happen to us."

"Why what happened to us?" asked Gail.

"Well, you know, the magical book, the fact that we live this unique experience, and that it is happening to us."

Gail smiled. "You still don't get it, do you?"

"What?" I asked, a little angry.

"It's not only happening to us, love," she said. "It is happening everywhere, in every corner of the world. Haven't you seen the expressions in the faces of the people we have met on all the islands we have visited? Maybe it was easier for us to relate to Alec and Sophie because we basically share the same dreams. Still, to others, it is happening differently. Don't you remember what was happening in the cities? A lot of middle-aged people are retiring early, or at least changing to part-time jobs. Buying that Harley Davidson, a campervan or that boat they had always dreamt of. Not because they value them as material possessions, but because of the places, they can take them to discover? Don't you see how many more people take longer holidays, regardless of their career or financial future? Parents are spending more quality time with their children and their grandchildren. Don't you realize what we have done for the last eight months?"

I saw her eyes glowing like embers in the night.

"I have an answer to your question," I said.

"Tell it to me because you know I know what you are going to say," said Gail.

I took her hand and then gave her a kiss.

"We are living our life to the fullest," I said. "I feel that I am living a thousand lives at the same time."

"Yes, love," Gail replied. "Many people are starting to live their life to the fullest, each in their unique way. I think we are starting to realize that we only have this unique and precious life we have been blessed with and that every second count in building a life full of purpose, of meaning."

The silence that came after our conversation was unique, as there was nothing else to say. This conversation with Gail had started in a heated mood. But at no time had we tried to hurt the other by expressing our thoughts, as we had done so often in the past. We had learned to think differently and, at the same time, respect each other, protected by the true love we felt. Gone were the meaningless discussions that had only one purpose: to hurt each other, which had almost destroyed our relationship. We had learned to love each other in every way that a person can love another, and it felt good. In the small world of "Distant Winds" and our dreams, we had found the true light that we had been searching so anxiously. Alight that symbolically connected with millions of other human beings around the world.

We hugged each other for a long time, just absorbing the energy that came from the truth we had just discovered. And, of course, we knew what would happen next.

We felt a soft breeze coming from the west, and for some reason, we knew this would be the last time during our trip that the book Thomas Blake had given to us would open.

We stared at the page, but this one instead of a poem had a short story. We read it in silence:

Far from the madding crowd

I went to the woods to rest my soul,

at the side of a living waterfall.

"What are you doing in this beautiful night of stars?" the waterfall asked.

"Resting my soul," the stranger replied.

"Resting your soul? From what?" asked the living waterfall.

"You wouldn't understand," said the resting man. "Just thank the mountains and the creek that holds you here, far away from it all, where your music can calm my soul."

The waterfall kept quiet for a while, thinking, then said: "Indeed, you should thank the mountains and the creek for not holding you anywhere. You have been blessed with the right of choice, and you can come and go as you wish, yet your soul needs to rest? I wish I could travel with you to see the madding crowds to see where you have come from."

I never forgot the words of the waterfall.

A year went by. The worst drought in memory withered the woods of the island where I once went to rest my soul. When I went back to the woods that year, the creek had dried up, and in the place where the singing waterfall had once sung, only the cold and dry stone remained.

"Do not be sad for the waterfall," said the distant wind, "for the cloud that now gives you shade is indeed the waterfall. Learn to see things with real light, and you will be blessed with understanding. The waterfall has discovered her choices, and now that she has become a cloud, she will eventually turn into rain, and who knows? After traveling through the madding crowds, maybe she will again want to become a living waterfall, for, in creation, we all have choices. The act of choosing will give us meaning.

"So, where do I belong in this timeless cycle?" the stranger asked.

"You should look again at all the things you have learned. Observe and understand the things that are happening around you. They are all part of *you, and you a part of them. Then you will be able to make a choice."*

I realized what the distant wind had said. That to find my real purpose, with the right understanding and no limitations, I would have to seek it.

As I stared towards the sky, I could see the living waterfall dressed as a white cotton ball, and the rain started pouring over me. "It's the living waterfall," I thought. Indeed, as the distant wind has said, "all is one."

So the stranger quietly returned to the madding crowds, to where he belonged, just as the rain became the creek where it belonged. He had discovered his purpose in life; to share with others the treasures he had found."

Thomas Blake

We kept silent for a while, tears in our eyes, imagining how he had been here before, long before us, being in the same boat, watching the same creek, and what he had felt and discovered by following his inner voice. The voice that came from his soul, and that now, as promised, was speaking to us, the lucky ones.

Gail was the first to speak.

"So, Thomas Blake discovered the true spirit of nature, and by discovering it, he realized who he really was."

"And what was that?" I asked.

"He knew he was a teacher, and that he had to spread the word of what he had seen, but in a very special way. He had to teach others that to be really free, there are some things you have to give up and that we have to see the world as it really is, and not as we sometimes think it is."

I kept quiet for a while, thinking.

"Well, I guess we have learned that not all of the things we want are necessarily the things we really need. So the important question here, Gail, is when is enough?"

"Hard to say," she said. "I guess the more advanced you get spiritually, the clearer the answer gets."

"Sometimes we spend more time thinking about what are we going to do with our annual holidays than planning what we will do with the rest of our lives. I guess that is the reason why sometimes life passes us by. We don't question our day-to-day routine. Instead of reaching out to discover a more exciting and fulfilling life by focusing ourselves on the big picture, we simply give up and go with the flow. We forget that there is a whole world out there waiting to be discovered, seen, and admired. We only have to give ourselves the time to perceive it."

XIX

Our journey was now coming to an end, as "Distant Winds" moved closer to New Zealand.

We left the Norfolk Islands with warm feelings. We had been treated like locals, sharing most of our stories with them and listening to their stories. "How easy it is to make friends anywhere when you honestly open yourself to others," I thought.

There was now no more land between our homeland and us. We sailed with a gentle breeze that made our journey home very pleasant at first. But later, as we stared at the open ocean, we stare at it with open hearts. No longer was it an immense mass of water; it was a new friend, one we would never lose.

We knew that once on dry land, we would miss these moments of magical solitude that we now have gotten so used to, despite our fears at the beginning of our journey. We were a little scared because we would never be the same. It would be impossible to go back and think the way we used to. Now that we had seen the world with our own eyes guided by a magical book given to us by an exceptional man who wanted to share with us all the beautiful experiences and things he had learned.

"What are we going to do, love?" Gail asked suddenly

"What do you mean?"

"What are we going to do with our lives? I know that deep within ourselves, we think the same, that we'll never be the same persons again, and that it'll be difficult to get used to the things we did before taking this journey. We won't see them with the same eyes."

The night was clear, full of bright stars, constellations popping out everywhere. God, how I had forgotten the stars, living in the light-polluted skies of the city! And here they were all, spangling and dense in the darkening air, the Southern Cross, the Crown's jewel, pointing southward, leading us back home.

"I guess we'll have to take one day at a time," I said. "Isn't that one of the things we've learned? Then, I guess, when the time comes to make a decision, we'll make it. We have now learned to be free, Gail. Free forever. And there shouldn't be any reason why we can't apply what we've learned on this trip to the world we are heading back to, or on any other parallel world. We will just have to use our instinct and imagination to combine the two worlds we now belong to."

" We're now fifteen-year dreamers in love again that just seem older on the outside, with more life behind us. But the child within us has flourished again, and now we can enjoy the simple things in life, and become true human beings. You have recaptured that glow in your eyes that comes from your soul, and that makes me love you every second of my life". She smiled, her eyes wet with tears.

The gentle breeze came once more from the west:

"The only risk

in life

is not to take

any risks

at all."

Gail and Michael

We looked at each other, as there was nothing else to say. We thought the book would not open again, but we had done it by ourselves. There, in the middle of the ocean, we just absorbed the wisdom of the moment. However, we knew that many things had to be answered by the future that awaited us, but one thing was for sure: we had fallen deeply in love once again. Not with our memories, but with the dreamers we had once again become.

XX

We were now 50 nautical miles from the port of Auckland, after sailing more than 6,000 nautical miles in a little less than a year.

Suddenly, in the middle of the night, we were awakened by a sudden change of weather conditions. The sea, smooth and tranquil when we went to sleep, seemed to be enraged. Waves were continually getting larger and larger and began hitting "Distant Winds" with unbridled fury. The sky, determined to aid the sea, formed a dark velvet cover of clouds, broken only by infrequent flashes of lightning. We had to arrive at the Bay of Auckland soon.

This abrupt change in weather wasn't merely a short squall, but seemed more like a strong thunderstorm, with immense waves thundering against the prow of our faithful "Distant Winds." The ocean seemed determined to prevent us from reaching our destination, and, we knew, this storm could only worsen. Since this was the first time we had experienced such a tempest in the open sea, we knew we were in trouble. We had to prepare for the worst.

"Gail, please take the wheel for a few minutes while I make contact with Auckland. Clip-on your safety harness while I get the life-jackets."

"Okay, love, but don't take too long," she said. Beneath the apparent calm of her voice, I could sense an undertone of anguish.

I went inside the cabin and tried to make contact with the port officials.

"Auckland, this is "Distant Winds," please come in."

Nothing. I tried it again.

"Auckland, this is "Distant Winds," please come in." "Maybe this is not the right frequency," I thought, adjusting the radio.

" 'Distant Winds,' this is the Auckland Maritime Authority. We can barely hear you."

"Auckland, thanks for answering. We are fifty nautical miles northeast of Auckland Bay. It seems there is a squall forming in front of us. We would like more details about the weather conditions…"

"What in God's name are you doing out there?" said the radio voice.

"Well, we are about to arrive in Auckland from the Indian Ocean."

A long silence came from the other side of the

line. " 'Distant Winds,' we issued a warning for boats this morning: strong winds and thunderstorms forming in the east, gradually moving out to sea."

He paused, then said: "They are heading straight towards you, 'Distant Winds.' There is nothing we can do under these conditions to help you. Please keep us informed, and don't forget to activate the emergency radio transmitter if you get in trouble."

"Roger, Auckland, we'll do so."

Then I heard a worried voice." Good luck 'Distant Winds.'"

"Thanks," I replied. "Now it is Gail and I alone again," I thought. "Don't panic," I said to myself. Keep calm and use the knowledge you have acquired on this trip. Although you have never faced a storm like this, it doesn't mean that you can't confront it."

I heard Gail screaming over the wind.

"Michael, please hurry up. I'm starting to get tired."

I grabbed the life jackets, activated the emergency beeper, took the all-weather toolkit, and rushed outside. The weather was deteriorating rapidly.

" Thanks, Gail, I'll take it from here," I said. "Please make sure that all ropes are tight, and check the rudder."

I secured the forehatch as well as all locker lids and windows. "All air vents are now sealed," I said to myself, and then turned back and secured all sliding hatches, making the cockpit totally waterproof.

We had experienced rough seas and short gale storms during our journey, but nothing like this. The ocean seemed to be flexing its muscles, and waves twelve-foot high tested the will of "Distant Winds," which was being pounded on all fronts. The full fury of the storm was now centered upon us, and in whatever direction we looked, we saw only more lightning and ever-growing waves. The rain began whipping down at painful speeds, our beloved "Distant Winds" being attacked on all fronts. I barely had time to clip on my safety harness when a wave lashed over onto the deck.

"Michael?"

"Yes, Gail?"

"I love you."

"I love you too, "I said.

"This is getting worse, right?"

I couldn't lie to her. "Yes, Gail, and it will get even worse. But we have to fight."

"I know," she said. "We had to scream at the top of our lungs, as our words were blown away by blasts of wind. The rain came down with such speed and strength that it was like being below a waterfall, continuous drop. The thrumming sound turned into one long constant thump.

Gail went down to the engine room to ensure that the pumps were working. She then came out again to the upper deck. I turned for a second towards her, and immediately sensed she was terrified.

"Michael, the lower deck is flooding!"

"Are the pumps working?" I asked.

"Yes, love, but they can't handle so much water."

"Okay, Gail, calm down. Go downstairs and start throwing away all the furniture and things that we don't need. That will give us more time to stay afloat."

"Okay, love." She stared at me.

"You know what I have just realized, Michael?" she said.

"What?"

"I'm not afraid to die. Dying here with you is not a sin. Not having lived life to the fullest would have been."

We looked at each other, and amidst the fury of the elements, we smiled. "Let's give it our best shot," I said.

The strong wind had now turned into a vicious gale. I frantically lowered the mainsail, leaving only the storm jib, a triangular scrap of canvas in the bow. The motor was running as strong as it could, and still, "Distant Winds" was struggling to maintain its course. Steering was almost impossible. We gibed, came aback, square waves leaped aboard, and water started to leak into the cockpit. Our safety harnesses, attached to a steel-mooring eye, saved us from being washed overboard. The keel was holding, but for how long? If it broke, that was it. We would spin round and round until a giant wave would sink us, and it would be the end. Most of all, there was no point in using our emergency raft. It wouldn't stand a chance in this storm.

Gail was getting exhausted, as she tried to throw all the furniture out of the boat to lighten "Distant Winds." I could see she was just about to give up.

Suddenly a "smooth" came. I knew because I had

read about it. It was a gap of a few seconds before the next huge wave arrived. I knew what I had to do.

"Gail, get into the cabin, now!"

"Michael, what are you saying? I won't leave you alone."

I looked at her. "Do it!" I said. "You will die out here. Turn the emergency beam on and stay there. Do it now!"

She looked at me. I knew she wanted to stay, but she also knew that she would die if she stayed outside any longer. The first signs of hypothermia were weakening her even more. She unlocked the lid and ran inside. I secured the top just before a huge wave crashed against "Distant Winds."

The immense strength of the wave jolted the wooden floor so strongly that I was thrown out of the boat. I plunged into the water, but only barely because of the safety harness. The ship leaned over to my side, not having been ready to handle such a disproportion of weight. My head was just above the wild churning water, and I needed to get out of there. I began pulling myself up by my safety harness, but a wave crashed against me and made me lose my footing. I started again, and just when my fingers held onto the deck, another wave hit from the opposite side. "Distant Winds" nearly capsized and stopped only a yard from hitting the water. I grabbed on with all my strength and prayed to God that it would straighten out. The moment it did, I hauled myself up and began straining against the winds to reach the mast.

I was about to panic. Is this the end? I thought. I could imagine Gail, terrified, praying for both of us. Would life prove that we had been wrong all the time and that we now finally had to face the reality of trying to do something beyond our limits?

But then, as I was just about to give up, there, through the rain that made visibility almost zero, I barely saw the figure of a man holding the storm jib firm, just when I had no strength left.

"Am I going crazy? Am I starting to see hallucinations?" I thought. I had heard this was one of the first signs of hypothermia and was convinced this was the beginning of the end. More than anything else, I wished I could spend these last moments with Gail, now that I had rediscovered her, to ask her to forgive me for not always being there for her. Then it wouldn't hurt so much.

But something extraordinary happened. The ghostly figure let the sail loose, making "Distant Winds" become more manageable. I desperately needed air and breathed in heavy, desperate gasps;

meanwhile, "Distant Winds" slowly righted itself, and was soon out of immediate danger.

The ghostly figure then turned to me and smiled, and I heard a familiar voice over the wind.

"Have a wonderful life, Michael."

I couldn't believe it.

"Mr. Blake?"

"Have a wonderful life, Michael," he said and then turned into the wind.

In that instant, a huge wave washed over the deck of "Distant Winds." When I was able to see again, he was gone.

I understood what he had meant. He had come to me at the exact moment I was about to give up. He was the hand I had felt so often throughout my life, since I was a child, helping me when I needed it the most. And suddenly, I realized I had to fight. The gentle wind that had so often shown us the world's magic was finally testing our determination and demanding a firm answer.

My panic disappeared, and a new strength I had never experienced before came from within me.

"I won't die today!" I shouted to the wind. "I will

live, and I will have a wonderful life."

I grabbed the steering wheel firmly.

An incredible peace came to me.

I had to fight.

***

"Michael, are you all right?"

I suddenly woke up.

"Gail?"

"Michael, are you okay?" Gail asked again.

I stared at her and at the sky. All the clouds that had been there before, determined to test our resolve, had disappeared. In their place was a pristine sky of a bright blue that met emerald green waters. All trace of our near-death experience had gone.

"What happened?" I asked her, regaining my consciousness.

"You beat the storm, love. It's been more than twelve hours since I left you up here. I thought it was all lost. Water started getting into the cabin, so I had to throw every piece of furniture and lose gear, as the pumps couldn't cope. And then I saw you shouting something to the wind. I went down again and locked the hatch and prayed for us. After a long time, I felt that the wind was dying and that the seas were getting calmer. I waited until a ray of sunlight came into the cabin, and I knew it was safe to open the hatch. Then I saw you, sitting where you were when I left you, holding the wheel, as though hypnotized, with a look in your eyes I had never seen before, Michael."

"What kind of look?" I asked.

"Like if you had seen something out of this world."

I stood up and stared at the calm horizon.

"I saw an angel, Gail."

"You saw what?"

"Never mind," I said. "I'll tell you some day."

She hugged me. "Thanks for saving our lives," she said.

I could barely speak, as my voice was breaking with emotion. I kissed her. I rested my head on her legs, with not a bit of physical strength left in me.

And before fainting again, I said:

"Never forget that we have to live a wonderful life, Gail. "Never."

EPILOGUE

Two weeks had gone by after arriving in Auckland from our journey.

We were fully recovered from our wounds and the storm, physically and emotionally. The New Zealand Coast guard, close to the Bay of Auckland's entrance, had rescued us. They were still at a loss as to how we had been able to survive such a storm. Nobody had survived before something like this before, and they could only tell us it was a miracle.

We went back to our old routine, looking for jobs, and although we were really trying, it was harder than we had thought. Still, we had decided not to hurry about our future plans, and to let the right moment arrive, when our hearts would tell us what to do next.

We thought it would be a good idea to get some of our old friends together for dinner to tell them about our trip. Gail called them, and they kindly accepted our invitation.

We served a delicious dinner based on all the exotic recipes we had learned on the islands using exotic spices and herbs, and how to use them to enhance a meal. We spoke about the trip, the incredible places we had seen, the people we had met, and the storm we had survived just before entering Auckland bay.

"So, did you bring back some souvenir from your trip Gail?" asked Peter, one of our friends.

"Well, not really," answered Gail. "Unfortunately, we lost almost all of our belongings in the storm. But we kept our most precious treasure with us."

"What is it?" Peter asked.

"Its a book with inspirational poems. Most of them were created during our trip."

"Can we see it?"

"Sure, why not?" Gail answered. She went into our bedroom and brought the wooden box. She then gave Peter the book containing all the lessons that had meant so much to us. As the book was passed from friend to friend, they started to look amazed, not knowing what to say.

"Is there something wrong?" I asked.

Everyone was quiet.

Suddenly Peter started laughing. The rest of the guests followed.

"Is this a joke?" Peter asked.

"What do you mean?" I said without understanding.

"What do I mean?" Peter said. "Come and look for yourself."

I took the book from his hands and showed it to Gail. We opened it:

It is easy in the world to follow the world's opinions;

it is easy in solitude to follow our own;

but the great man is hewho in the midst

of the crowd keeps with perfect sweetness the

independence of solitude.

"Emerson," I said.

"Correct," said Gail.

***

In the silence of the room, I stared at Gail. She stared at me too. We barely listened to what our friends were about to say because they still couldn't see it.

"Good joke, Michael, Gail!" Peter said. "There is no doubt that you have learned to prepare exotic and exquisite meals. We know you had a long and wonderful trip, but we didn't know that you had also learned to read books that contain only empty pages!" The room exploded in laughter.

***

We went back to the pier where we first met "Distant Winds," where this magical adventure had begun. Mr. Roberts offered to repurchase it, now that it had proved to be a seaworthy boat, and his offer was generous. We had finally returned "Distant Winds" to Mr. Roberts, though not without first taking a last deep breath in its upper deck. A final goodbye to a friend who did so much for us, without asking anything in return. "Friends such as "Distant Winds" are tough to find in these times we live," I thought. And although we were very sad to sell it, we knew that this would definitely not be its last journey on the open seas.

"Remember what we said to Mr. Roberts about "Distant Winds," Gail?"

"Sure," she replied. "It was a good idea to tell him that we never named it. Maybe this way, the next owners will see with true eyes what the boat means, without knowing its real name. That the'll have to discover for themselves."

"Yeah," I said. "I've learned that nobody can own "Distant Winds," but she can truly take you to beautiful places and help make your dreams come true."

Gail sat down. She looked sad.

"I feel very lonely," Gail said.

"I feel lonely too, love. It seems that our friends can't understand what we have really learned on this trip. This journey has changed and enriched our lives, and I guess it is our duty to at least share with others what we have seen and experienced. We now need to learn how to share this knowledge with others that are also searching. People who think like us and are just waiting for a signal to take the jump. The same way Thomas Blake helped us."

"And how will we do that?" Gail asked.

An idea came to mind. "Maybe we should write a book about the trip. Share with others our adventures, the places we have discovered, and the lessons we have learned by broadening our own horizons. Share the thoughts of the friends that helped us, and the ones we discovered by ourselves. Put it in writing so that others can see how an experience like this can bring together two persons again, forever". I stopped, then stared at my beautiful Gail:

"Now I know for sure that anyone can do what we have done, love, make dreams come true, and become better persons, each in our own and unique way.

"A book," Gail said. "I think that's a great idea. What should we call it?"

"There is only one way to name it love. You know that as well as I do."

She looked at me and then smiled.

"So 'Distant Winds' it shall be called!" said Gail.

The book that had now become our best teacher opened once again.

The real voyage in life consists not only in seeking new worlds, but in seeing your own with true eyes.

We kept staring at each other.

"Blake," I said.

"Correct," answered Gail.

We kept silent for a while. Gail spoke first.

"Michael?"

"Yes, love?"

"It's the last page of the book."

"I know," I said. "This book has already helped us enough. Now it's us alone, and our love. The real you and me."

"I know," Gail answered. "You didn't need to say it." She paused and then gazed at the horizon. "Do you think there will be more people like Alex and Sophie? More like Thoreau, Emerson, Blake, and all the others? More like us?"

"Oh, yes. I have no doubts now," I said. "Now, I'm sure you can find people dreaming their own dreams in every corner of the world."

"That's good to know," said Gail. The world is finally turning into a more spiritual place. More and more people are learning to appreciate the real treasures of life, the ones that can't be bought, or sold."

I placed the book inside the wooden box and closed the lid. In that instant, a couple that had been walking up and down the pier approached us.

"Excuse me, sir," said the girl.

"Yes?"

"Do you know who owns the boat shop at the end of the pier?"

"Yes," I said. "It's Mr. Roberts. Why? Are you planning to buy a boat?"

"Well, yes," said the young man. "We are planning to take a long trip."

Gail smiled. "Tired of the daily routine, and needing a change in your life? "

"Yes," said the girl, a little surprised by my

openness. "We want to see other worlds to discover who we really are, you know?"

Gail smiled.

"Oh, yes, we do know."

"What's your name?" Gail asked the thin, red-haired girl.

"I'm Debbie, and this is my boyfriend, Sam."

Gail looked at me. I smiled. "You do it," I said

"Well, Debbie, Sam," said Gail, "this may sound strange because we have just met you, but Michael and I would like to give you a present for your trip. You just have to promise us two things: that you won't open it until you are at sea, and that whatever happens..."

***

I hugged Gail in silence, not knowing precisely what the future would bring, but confident that we had each other and that we had taken hold of our lives, of our love.

It was then when I heard a voice coming from

within. I reached for my journal and my pen, and began to write:

"*In my beautiful birthplace of New Zealand is Auckland, the largest city in an emerald green country, often referred to as "the land of the long cloud." Auckland itself is surrounded by lush green rolling hills. It is the majestic Bay of Auckland, where sailing boats arrive whispering tales of distant lands. Others depart in search of magic worlds.*"

The sun started to fade on the horizon, an explosion of colors covering the sky. We sat silently and watched the world around us. We weren't teenagers anymore, nor were we old people. It really didn't matter. Just as the very old and the very young know, we had finally learned to sit next to one another and not say anything, and still feel content in the wonder of our silence. We were one now, the sum of our parts bigger than the parts themselves. And as I kept writing, I heard a whisper coming from the sea:

Have a wonderful life...

ABOUT THE AUTHOR

Sergio Bambarén Roggero was born on the first day of December of 1960 in Lima, Peru. Educated in a British School, Sergio was captivated from his early years by the sea, having been born in a city that meets the ocean. This bond would influence him for the rest of his life, and put him in a journey he would never expect: to become a writer. His traveling spirit took him to the U.S.A., where he graduated as a Chemical Engineer at Texas A&M University. However, the ocean was still his greatest love, so he went surfing to places like Central America, Mexico, California, and Hawaii. After a brief stay in the country where he was born, Sergio decided to migrate to Sydney, Australia, where he worked as a Sales Manager for a multinational company. However, he also managed to travel to Southeast Asia and African coasts in search of the perfect wave. Legendary places like Bali, Nias, Jeffrey's Bay, Agadir in Morocco, the Philippines, and Australia and New Zealand were part of his surfing travels. After several years in Australia, Sergio took a sabbatical year and traveled to Europe in search of the perfect wave. It was in Portugal, on a beautiful beach surrounded by pine forests called Guincho, where Sergio found the purpose of his life and a very special friend while surfing: a lonely dolphin that inspired him to write his first novel: "The Dolphin, Story of a Dreamer". After he returned to Sydney, his book was published in Oz in 1996. He sold more than 100,000 copies of "The Dolphin" in Australia in less than a year. "The Dolphin" has now been translated into more than 40 languages and dialects. His books have been published in more than seventy countries.

www.sbambaren.com

www.sergiobambarenblog.com

www.facebook.com/SergioBambaren.official.site/

https://instagram.com/sergio_bambaren

Twitter: @sbambaren

Email: office@sergiobambarenblog.com

YouTube: Sergio BAMBAREN ROGGERO

Best-sellers by Sergio Bambaren:

- *The Dolphin, story of a dreamer*
- *Beach of Dreams*
- *Distant Winds*
- *Samantha*
- *The story of Bow*
- *Tales from the Heavens*
- *Crystal River*
- *The Story of the Starfish and the mule*
- *The Blue Grout*
- *The Rose of Jericho*
- *Angels of the Ocean*
- *The Dolphin and the waves of life*
- *Letters to my son Daniel*
- *The Best is yet to come!*
- *The Guardian of the Light*

- *The time of the whales.*
- *A promise is a promise*
- *The Beating heart of the desert*
- *The Sound of Silence*
- *The House of Light*
- *Chiqui*
- *Live your dreams!*
- *The Light at the other side of the river*
- *The Messenger – A fable (2020)*

Book Rights:

Mertin-Litag Literary Agency,

Frankfurt

info@mertin-litag.de

serbambaren@gmail.com

Made in United States
Orlando, FL
20 May 2022

18039609R00120